FREEING ME

LOSING MY RELIGION TO FIND GOD

FREEING ME: LOSING MY RELIGION TO FIND GOD
Copyright © 2014 by Civitas Press

ISBN #978-0692303696
Published by Civitas Press, LLC
San Jose, CA,
www.civitaspress.com

Disclaimer

The author has taken all steps to ensure that every aspect of this story is true and that any misrepresentation was unintentional.

I have tried to recreate events, locales and conversations from my memories of them. In order to maintain their anonymity, in some instances I have changed the names of individuals and places. I may have changed some identifying characteristics and details such as physical properties, occupations and places of residence.

Serena,
Thanks for listening & carrying over
these last few years.
Peace & Love,

FREEING ME

LOSING MY RELIGION TO FIND GOD

TRAVIS KLASSEN

CivitasPress

Publishing inspiring and redemptive ideas.[sm]

ENDORSEMENTS FOR "FREEING ME"

"The number of stories of people leaving the confines of religion to save their faith continues to grow. People are waking up and listening to the deep call of God in their soul. They are making brave but terrifying choices to leave all that is familiar behind in search of a faith that is more real and free than what they found through years in church. Travis Klassen's honest and raw story will encourage many on their road toward leaving religion but restoring their faith. It will help many feel less alone, less crazy, and more sure that freedom is worth fighting for."

Kathy Escobar, Co-Pastor of The Refuge and author of *Faith Shift: Finding your Way Forward When Everything You Believe is Coming Apart*

"It is indeed tragic that a story like Freeing Me must be told. Tragic because there is in place a deeply-rooted religious system that feeds a power and money driven machine that often rolls over questioning people in its pathway. Travis bares his heart with candor and grace. After reading this book, Henri Nouwen's words burned in my heart: 'One thing is clear to me: The temptation of power is greatest when intimacy is feared. Much Christian leadership is exercised by people who do not know how to develop healthy, intimate relationships and have opted for power and control instead. Many Christian empire builders have been people unable to give and receive love.' Travis was under the thumb of a leader like this. Freeing Me chronicles his exodus out of controlled religion into a freedom where love reigns. I cannot recommend this book highly enough."

Jon Zens, author of *58 to 0 -- How Christ Leads Through the One Anothers*

"Freeing Me is a wrenching story of faith, disillusionment, and hope. With simple, straightforward prose Klassen opens up his chest and shares some of his most painful moments with us. It is a story that is all to familiar to so many, but reading it I was reminded that I am not alone."

Micah J. Murray, Blogger at RedemptionPictures.com

Klassen's story isn't as rare as we'd like to believe. Freeing Me is an emotionally honest account proving how serving God can be the most powerful force to free or enslave us. Follow Klassen into the slippery deception of spiritual abuse and his trail of crumbs and tears to get out--soul and family intact.

Dale & Jonalyn Fincher, authors, founders of Soulation, and guides of the FreedomBuilders, a community of ragamuffins for spiritual healing (soulation.org/freedombuilders).

DEDICATION

To my best friend, my soul mate, and my lover: Veronica, you've been amazing throughout this journey. Your heart has been broken, healed, broken and healed so many times...and yet our love is stronger than ever.

To my daughters, Topanga & Tehillah: You may not even know how much you played a part in all of this. Because we knew there was more, there was something more authentic out there, and we went to find it. We stopped running around like crazy people because you matter more to us than ministry. I can see heaven in your eyes.

To my son, Drake: Our dreams for you were birthed of our desire to understand the divine nature of a God who fathers and mothers the lost, rejected & abandoned. Adoption is one of the truest ways we could walk out our faith. When you walked into our home, Love walked in with you.

To the broken, to the searching, to the "rebels," to the followers of Jesus: Be encouraged. Wherever you are on the journey, may peace flood your soul and may love make you whole. Remember, wherever love is, God is there also.

CONTENTS

ACKNOWLEDGEMENTS

The readers of Churchburned.com and TravisKlassen.com – You've been a very real part of this journey. Your feedback, encouragement and pushback have caused me to keep searching. Thank you for your support.

Kathy Klassen – You were the first person to be given a copy of my very first draft. The wise words and cautious criticism that you offered in response were integral to the raw honesty now contained in the following pages. Thank you.

Inge Anderson – Your indelible influence on my writing is apparent on multiple levels. Thank you for your valuable feedback.

Russ Klassen – Thanks for reading one of my first passes – in a night! I've enjoyed talking through some of this stuff with you.

Stacey & Joe Malleck – You've both been great friends to Veronica & I, one of the few who stuck with us as we asked questions and pushed boundaries. Thank you for reading some of my earliest drafts and supporting this laborious process.

Matt Schoberg – You are a great friend. I know blog stats, Facebook likes and Twitter followers don't really matter to you, and I treasure this. Thanks for being there.

Steve Klassen – I am so thankful for the way we can go six months without speaking and then just pick up right where we left off. Thank you for your incredible generosity, in producing "Chase The Dark Away," a song written along the journey.

Frank Schaeffer – When you agreed to write the foreword for this book, I laughed with joy. Your story was one of the reasons I chose to share mine. Thank you for your gracious words.

Amy Mitchell – I've always loved your work, so having you critique and proofread mine was an honor. Thank you for your empathetic support of this project.

Mom & Dad, Ben, Katie, Jana & my entire extended family – That I took this journey made some of you uncomfortable, yet I've always felt your love, support and acceptance. Thank you.

Jonathan Brink – A coach, counselor, editor and friend. Had I not found you, this journey would likely not have been possible, and though even if it were, it would not have been as rich an experience. Thank you for making me go beyond my limits. You taught me about redemption and helped me find it.

Veronica – You've lost sleep, you've listened to me read aloud for hours, you've pushed back and pushed yourself beyond where you'd ever thought you'd go…and yet here we are, together. Thank you for being the most creatively supportive, brutally honest, loving, passionate, expressive person I know. You've made my life so much more amazing. I love you.

FOREWORD

Religion is a neurological disorder and faith is the only cure. Faith can't exist without doubt.

For many who were raised fundamentalist evangelical circles, the rules of this brand of Christianity were all that mattered. We did not know that faith can and must be challenged. And our addiction to certainty spread to politics. When you are sure you are right those who question aren't just wrong but evil.

Neuroscience has proved that the brain is malleable. Brains change because of the environments they're grown in. Playing a musical instrument grows a brain differently than the brains of non-musicians. Vets' brains are different after the stress of combat. These changes show up on scans. They are physical and real. Religious belief changes brains too.

The legion of home schooled, Christian school graduates, Christian college graduates and others raised in the Never, Never Land of evangelical non-questioning of myth have launched themselves into the political process. The very fact that the facts point in the opposite direction than they want to go is proof to them they are right.

Religion spends millions brainwashing its own to believe a specific myth of the origins of the universe, while ensuring its own survival by weaving the need for religion into the creation story. Fundamentalist belief grows brains incapable of dealing with the world as it actually is. Tribesmen in Borneo, eating the heart of an enemy and believing that they will thereby gain his strength, and Tea Party evangelical Republicans believing that America is special, the Bible is true also believe that they're martyrs whenever they encounter people who question their "facts."

Being raised in a home where you're taught from birth – as I was as the son of evangelical missionaries -- that the evidence of your eyes and ears is wrong, that, for instance, unseen forces are fighting over the destiny of your soul, that whatever science, the local newspaper or your teacher says to the contrary, the earth is young, changes your brain. Delusion leads to more delusion, unless something helps you snap out of it.

Thus the "world's way" is always suspect. So 2 plus 2 can't equal 4 because the New York Times thinks it does! That's "worldly wisdom" i.e., a fact. And facts are bad.

Enter home school moms protecting their children from information. Enter people who fear questions.

In this book, Travis tells the story of his journey of being born, raised, indoctrinated and of eventually rising to prominence in a fundamentalist church. This is a story that in another context I lived. We both traveled from non-questioning to questioning.

The religious establishment from whence we came focuses its attention inward on itself, its primary aim based on self-preservation. Everything it needs to be self-sustaining is found within the confines of the bubble it creates. There is a subset of every major component of culture that simply adds a "Christian" prefix for sanitization: Christian entertainment, Christian education, Christian media etc.

In this book dogmatic, morality-based theology is being replaced by open and honest conversation. Fear is being conquered by love.

Whether God is a man on a throne made of gold or a divine force of love that surrounds, where there is love, where there is beauty, where there is peace; it is there that our religion fades and is replaced with faith.

Frank Schaeffer, August 21, 2014

PREFACE

To the brokenhearted, the ones who've stayed in abusive religious environments, and to the ones who've left. To the ones who've loved God and felt the presence of Love and Peace and to the ones who just haven't.

I've heard so many of your stories, your complicated journeys in, out and through the "institutional" church. Whether you are living out your need for community in a big building or in a home, whether you feel found or lost, we are all brothers and sisters. We are the Church.

Maybe you feel like you're on "the outside" or even just the fringe. Whether you've just found yourself there or whether you intentionally destined yourself there, know this: you are not alone.

You are not wrong for asking questions, you are not wrong for looking for God beyond the box. We're human, and that makes us family.

You've likely been wounded. When you put forty or fifty of us in a room, you're gonna hear some pretty messy stuff. Your story is beautiful, whether tragic or triumphant. Tell it.

We all have a story.

Here's mine.

1

BETRAYAL

We'd later describe this night as one of the worst of our lives.

My wife was now crying so hard that she had to excuse herself to the restroom and try to gather her composure, or at least make an attempt to protect her self-worth, let alone salvage any dignity she had left. She continued to sob as she shut and locked the door behind her and crumbled to the floor.

We had just discovered that the church we'd planted and co-pastored would no longer be home. In a moment, everything we had imagined and hoped for had been stripped away. I would no longer be a worship pastor.

"God!?" Veronica would later tell me she felt her heart screaming as she gasped for air. "I'm not going to make it! What's going on? Why is this happening to us?"

Eight feet away from her, the white porcelain bowl beckoned her near, and she felt the cold hard tile moving beneath her as she crawled towards it, her body convulsing with a physical expression of her emotional pain.

The scornful silence in the room she'd vacated moments ago was shattered by the sound of her body expelling whatever it could to accommodate the unbearable anxiety that was being forced into her. The painful retching sound permeated the four-inch wall that physically separated her from the pain, the hurt, and the hate that filled the room in which I sat and waited.

We'd been told this meeting had been called with the intention of initiating relational restoration. That turned out to be a lie. We had been set up for banishment.

Veronica and I had recently begun a sabbatical from our duties at the church, taking a much-needed break from ministry brought on by sheer exhaustion. In the five weeks since we'd announced our desire to rest and refocus, my relationship with Pastor Ken, the church's senior leader and my best friend, had diminished greatly.

To say the meeting wasn't going well for us would be an understatement. Our pastor had just accused me of insubordination. He had elaborated by explaining that I was no longer on board with the vision of the church. This was true. I had reached my end with his personal vision. But it was not true that I had abandoned the original vision, one which saw people deeply connected together in community worshipping God.

It was this statement that had chased Veronica into the powder room. If anyone knew of the dedication and commitment I had for our pastor's original vision, it was she. I'd basically missed the first few years of our daughter's lives because I'd given nearly every hour of my life not spent sleeping, eating or working my day job to serve in the church.

We had actually come to the meeting with hopeful anticipation of working through the stress and misunderstanding that had become apparent in the relationship between Pastor Ken and myself. Veronica had great faith. She believed since we were all Christians, "everything would just have to work out!"

Unfortunately, her hopes were not realized.

The conversation instead followed a template similar to many I'd previously been involved in but where I'd had a seat on the other side of the room.

Without speaking, we waited for Veronica to return. It was an awkward silence, one that filled the room with a noxious angst. I sat across from former trusted advisors, mentors, confidants and friends. For four minutes and thirty seconds we lingered in quiet tension, waiting for my wife to return before resuming the confrontation, our eyes dancing a clumsily choreographed routine of avoidance. I remember specifically admiring a portion of the wall for about half of that time, as if it were the only wall I'd ever seen painted in that particular shade of beige. Or was it taupe? Perhaps creme? It didn't matter. It earned my undivided attention for at least one hundred and twenty seconds on that painful evening.

I stole quick, fleeting glances across the expanse of the living room at the couple I'd grown to love, cherish, honor and respect over the last eight years, trying to comprehend how we got to this point and what was really going on. Surely, this wouldn't actually be the end, would it? We'd spent so much time together, in ministry and as friends, what issue could arise that would result in such an impasse?

The silence was deafening and spoke volumes of the current state of my relationship with the people I sat across from. There was a clear line separating "us" from "them." On one side of the room sat our pastor's wife, Diane, a tiny waif of a woman who barely filled half a cushion of the couch she occupied alone. She always struck me as a nervous woman. She was sweet and submissive, comfortable playing a supporting role to the electrifying character her husband portrayed.

Pastor Ken sat next to her, reclining in his lazy-boy rocker and tossing his shoulder length blonde hair impatiently as we all endured this brief intermission from the madness. He reminded me of an agitated lion, his mane flowing this way and that, his anger barely contained beneath the unsettled golden sea. It was excruciating to be at odds with the man I'd served, the man I'd loved as a leader and friend, and be unwilling to waver from my stance, from a perspective so different from his.

As I continued to ponder in the temporary silence of the room, I had flashbacks of better days, so many better days that seemed infinitely more positive than the one we were creating now. My pastor was just sitting there, wearing white socks and navy blue slippers—the same slippers I'd seen him wear many times before, like when our families shared breakfast together or when we'd stay late and watch a movie. We'd been like family, so this night was a long, painful, heart-wrenching experience for all of us.

To the left of Ken and his wife sat Luke and Rachel, the head elder and his wife. It was the four of them versus the two of us. We were clearly and intentionally outnumbered. The only person in our entourage was my dad, whom I had brought along for moral support. This may have actually been a mistake on my part. My dad was a board member and an old friend of Ken's. He stayed quiet for the most part, helpless to do much beyond observing the emotional devastation occurring right before his eyes. My dad is a peacemaker at heart, but in this place there was no peace to be found.

When my wife finally returned, she sat at my feet, her eyes void of life and swollen from the countless tears she'd cried in the solace of the powder room. Together, we maintained strong eye contact with the floor, looking across the room by tracing the lines of the planks in the hardwood and then making the brave climb upwards to look into the faces of our accusers, our adversaries, as they spoke.

The elders and senior pastor were vigorously making their case, providing evidence to each other, demonstrating our insubordination, incompetency and history of poor communication. It was as if we were the audience in a kangaroo court, with no right to speak or defend ourselves. It wouldn't have made a difference. They used hundreds of verbal paragraphs to illustrate just how wrong, how "out of line" we'd become.

Much of the dialogue sounded like a dull and muffled roar as we sat there and took blow after blow. A few words here and there really hit the mark, penetrating through whatever guards we had left and wounding us to the depths of our beings. The emotional shock was causing me great distraction and making it difficult to keep track of the conversation that seemed to be fading in and out.

Sitting in the seat of the broken was nearly unbearable. I found my mind wandering, trying to find solace in the storm.

Our pastor's home was perched on the side of a mountain with a panoramic view of the entire city. I remember looking out the grand picture windows, his diatribe continuing in the background, and observing a heavy fog roll in that obstructed the view of the valley below. The beautiful city lights slowly faded to grey as the fog thickened, leaving me to see nothing but the man whom I'd once loved as a father, still talking, reflected in the glass.

I remained attentive enough to hear Pastor Ken assert that I had been challenging the way things were being done and that "We can't have our leadership questioning the senior leader." Luke, the head elder, added, "There is no room for doubt here." It felt like I was being crushed.

I couldn't help but recount to myself how much he had forgotten our original vision, the one that had launched our ministry in the first place. Where was that evidence? Where was the remembrance of a community that was deeply passionate about God, deeply connected together? None of that was brought up.

Our pastor made it clear that if we didn't immediately cease questioning the way things were done and return to a position of submission under his authority, we'd be on our own, spiritually speaking—left all alone to fend for ourselves in a scary world.

"You'll be stepping into a very dangerous place," he said. "You'll be outside of the covering of this house." I couldn't tell if his last words were meant to be a literal statement or a spiritual one.

Yes, the man with the long blonde hair who'd been speaking for nearly an hour now was both our landlord and our senior pastor. Our family had rented the basement suite two floors down from where we were all currently sitting. During the course of this distressing conversation, once we made it clear we weren't going to beg for their forgiveness and "turn from our rebellious and insubordinate ways," we were handed an eviction notice from the petite woman sitting on half a couch cushion across the room.

Talk about getting kicked while you're down.

We weren't really given a chance to defend ourselves or even defend our position on some of the matters for which we found ourselves on trial. I'm confident that had we buckled, we would have survived. It was almost as if we simply had to break.

The pressure to give in was nearly enough to cause me to cry uncle and fall back into line. Even though it felt like they were trying to break my spirit, I knew the people seated across from us weren't evil. They were part of a system that had ways to deal with rogue thinkers and lost sheep. A little discipline and discipleship and they were certain we could be rehabilitated.

I knew what we had to do to avoid being cast out, but it didn't make sense. I had been going against my own convictions for too long. For me, the duality of who I was trying to be as a pastor and who I was as person following Jesus was pulling me apart.

All we had to do was say the words. Submit. Bow the knee. And this I just couldn't do. I had too much integrity to give up now.

Our pastor had made crystal clear, during the five or so challenging weeks that preceded this awful night, "I'm fine if you write, but if you write 'against' the church, you will no longer be welcome in our home." I guess that's where the eviction notice tied into it all. He must have perceived my blog posts to be too inflammatory to ignore.

My blog's content and subject matter was nothing unfamiliar to Pastor Ken. I had been charged by Ken to grow the ministry through sharing a heavy social media presence, including my blog. We'd formed our church together based on the premise it would be different than most, and the blog was a way to communicate that. But it had become obvious to me that over the last couple of years our original vision had been completely lost. His stance on church doctrine and various social issues had devolved to a more closed, traditional view, while my thoughts had only continued to become more liberal, open and progressive. It was clear that Ken and I were moving in different directions. My blog became a space to share that conviction.

We'd been given a choice. After years of dedication and respectful submission it had all come down to this: "It's my way or the highway," he would have said, had we just cut through the spiritual rhetoric and agreed to have an open and honest conversation. This long, drawn-out meeting could have been over much sooner. I'm confident he believed everything holy, true and honorable was on his side.

And had we been able to set aside the formalities and engage in frank conversation, I would have replied "Well, I guess it's time for a road trip," sarcastically but honestly. Then, knowing I was choosing the highway over his way, I would have stood and frantically tried to find my keys, ready to embrace the freedom of the open road.

Indeed, after some time, I did stand, for the first time in the three-hour meeting, and I knew this was the last time I would grace his home. I had taken a stand for my heart, my family, and myself, and it was good. I had chosen the path of honesty, and as hard as it was to chart, it was good. Veronica and I exited, this time through the front door and around the back, instead of taking the inside stairs like we usually did. I held the eviction letter in my hand, rolled and crumpled in the middle where I grasped it firmly, wondering where we'd go.

We slowly walked down the twenty-six wooden stairs on the southeast side of the house. Both Veronica and I were shell-shocked and speechless. I had a dull, numbing headache as we opened the door to our suite, trudged to our bedroom and collapsed on the bed, broken.

2

EVICTION

The night following our meeting was a nearly a sleepless one. I remember looking over at the iridescent glow of the alarm clock next to our bed at nearly two in the morning, both Veronica and me still awake, processing the words that had been spoken and the way the events of the evening had transpired. We had only traveled 20 feet to our basement apartment, but it felt like we were a world away.

As we lay in bed, we replayed the events of the evening over and over again.

Even though I'd felt a spark of hope going into the meeting as a result of Veronica's optimism that our shared faith would result in a peaceful resolve, I had prepared resignation letters just in case.

I had never wanted to actually deliver them. I had wanted to allow my verbal request to suspend my responsibilities to stand and then take the summer to rest and reevaluate how we fit inside the church and how the church fit with us.

We'd been given a choice: We'd been asked to align or resign. In a moment, we were forced to choose to either cease questioning the way things were being done in the church we co-founded and co-led or leave quietly. We needed to be free to discover who we were meant to be.

Although I had chosen to find a way to stay in the conflict and change of vision, Veronica could clearly see the power struggle and the emotional and spiritual abuse. For the first time, I could no longer mindlessly follow or submit to Ken's spiritual guidance as he so desperately pleaded with me to do.

Hours earlier, it had become clear that I could not have it both ways. If I wanted to think, to question, to discover, I would have to separate from the man whom I had installed as the spiritual authority over my life.

Once I realized the submissive words expected by our senior pastor weren't going to cross my lips, I reached into my bag and passed two letters to the man to whom only three years earlier I had made a covenant to serve for the rest of my life. The first letter tendered my resignation from the board of directors and the second from my position as Senior Associate Leader.

Drafting my letters had taken most of the day leading up to the traumatic meeting. I agonized over the smallest of details. I had driven to an office supply store in town to select just the right paper on which to compose my letters of leave.

While holding my letters, unopened, Pastor Ken had looked to the elders and then over at his wife, Diane, and nodded. She reached behind her to the end table that sat next to the couch then stood and crossed to where we still sat. Without making eye contact with us, she delivered an envelope of her own containing the letter that would detail our fate, a symbolic gesture of support and defense of her husband. Because we had chosen to hold on to our integrity over mindless submission, we'd been handed an eviction notice, a single-page, double-spaced letter that actually felt like a request for divorce.

I'm pretty sure Diane is the one who actually drafted and typed up the eviction notice, as it was written in a style unlike that which I'd come to know from Pastor Ken. It seemed hastily drafted, was written in large print (the font size was at least 14 or 16 pts), and contained several grammatical errors. I had the feeling Ken wouldn't have wanted to sully his own conscience, so he likely delegated the task to his wife.

Looking back, I would have called Pastor Ken my best friend. Or at least I thought we'd been close friends. History suggested that interpretation. However, our pastor informed both the board of directors and myself that we were only close because of our business relationship, the joint venture of operating the successful ministry we'd built from the ground up. Any semblance of friendship was an illusion that would cease, should I choose to terminate my involvement in the day-to-day operations of the ministry.

The accusation jarred me. Had I so completely misread the relationship? Had our countless moments of shared intention, dreaming and building something for God been untrue? Running around Disney World in Florida, riding the Aerosmith roller coaster over and over again, just the two of us, playing hooky from a ministry conference session, felt more like friendship than business partnership. Our weekly Monday night meetings, drinking rum &cokes until late and talking about anything and everything, had led me to believe I was hanging out with a lifelong friend.

Our relationship hadn't felt "all business" to me. I truly felt he was the spiritual father to me he claimed to be. Even as we were embroiled in tension, what father abandons his child just because they choose to hold onto an original vision, one that we had both agreed upon?

We'd co-founded the church together only three years earlier. From the beginning of our foray into ministry, we were out to make a name for ourselves. I remember the first service like it was yesterday, on a crisp, cool evening in May. Since that opening service, I'd spent significantly more time with Pastor Ken than I'd spent with my wife.

When speaking of Pastor Ken to each other, Veronica and I didn't even need to use his name; we simply referred to my spiritual father as "he" or "him." When I walked in the door after work for a quick moment with my family before heading to the church, Veronica could ask something like, "Did he get a hold of you?" or "Have you heard from him today?" and I would know exactly of whom she was speaking. I would later realize that I used the words "he" and "him" far more often in reference to our pastor than I did in reference to God.

Yes, we had our fair share of disagreements, but we were as close as family. Separation had never been an option. Although our arguments had been progressively getting worse, none of them had anything on the dispute in which we found ourselves embroiled. Most of our previous conflicts were over pretty minor issues, and I'd grown accustomed to voicing just the right amount of criticism before generally caving and letting him win. But this was different. I was challenging the very fabric of our collective vision. I was on the wrong side of the equation when it came to the shared vision of the church, one he accepted as fundamentally right. I was questioning, I was doubting, and perhaps worst of all, I was blogging.

I probably wasn't doing myself any favors by working through my theological quandaries in the open public forum of my blog. Every doubt, every idea, every differing perspective was out there for all to see. I was learning to be vulnerable, to take myself off the pedestal of ministry and allow myself to just "be."

When I first started blogging, I only wrote what I would consider to be encouraging words. I only wrote words of discovery, hope and faith. I wrote about "being instead of doing" and about "being real."

The words that were published on my blog would eventually be used against me to prove that I wasn't really on board with the vision of the church leadership. And the truth is, I wasn't. It had changed so radically from what we had originally intended, it would be dishonest of me to share the vision. Since I held a pretty prominent place on the church leadership, it was clear the words I was writing simply didn't dovetail with Pastor Ken's new vision.

Unity was very important to us as a leadership team, but in hindsight, unity at the cost of integrity is distorted and becomes control. As leaders, we were never to publically disagree or question our senior leader's thoughts, words or actions. Even in our highest-level staff meetings, rarely would a member of the leadership work up the courage to challenge Pastor Ken. If someone did speak out bravely, Pastor Ken wouldn't even have to defend himself; another member of his team would do it for him.

When Pastor Ken looked at our church, it seemed to me like he needed to assimilate, align, contain and control; a sort of imposed unity. When I looked at our church, I saw a beautifully vibrant, multifaceted assembly of Jesus' followers; diversity to be embraced and celebrated. It wasn't my intention to "write against" the church, but Pastor Ken read every word I wrote through his own lens.

There was one blog post in particular that really got Pastor Ken riled up. It was one of the first times I'd seen his neck turn red as the mane of blonde tossed in agitation. I'd been feeling inspired to write what I felt church was really all about, and I shared it with my limited audience. Although he stopped short of demanding I take the post down, he did warn me of the damage I could potentially cause.

I knew when I wrote it that the piece might offend more traditional proponents of church, but I also thought that Ken and I were united in a vision that differed from the traditional concept and practice of church. I'd written:

The church is (or should be) a group or community of people following Jesus. That's it.

Yes, the corporate gathering of believers is important, but not at the expense of a feet hitting the ground & kicking up dust kind of personal walk with God. Worship in a church setting is great, but how often do we worship God individually or with a small group of friends/fellow believers? Fellowship (for lack of a better word) is important, but we've got to make real time for for people, developing relationship & community with them. Accountability is important, but just how accountable are we, slipping in and slipping out of a group of three hundred believers on a Sunday morning.

We've learned to lean on the church (the institution) as a crutch, or maybe as a pill; a way for us to get all of our spiritual needs & obligations met & fulfilled in one place, in one or two hours. Get in, get 'er done, get out.

This is where I want to shift my mindset. Stop doing church, stop (merely) going to church, and start being the church. This is what we were called to be!

I wish you could hear my laughter as I write; excited, mischievous, nervous all at once. Ha ha! We are getting closer! Love God, and love people. Do it on your own time too, not just in a once-a-week, pre-allotted two hour time period. Amen. Obviously, I'll be writing more on what I think this means soon. Just stirring the pot for now...

The words were a testament to the discovery of a life-giving faith where there was once only room for a religion. The words were a declaration of freedom. I was writing words that celebrated what the church was meant to be.

These words would come to haunt me.

Our church. Our community. Our relationships. Life as we knew it. All of that had come to an end. When I began asking critical questions,

Pastor Ken apparently ceased to be a friend. As of the meeting that night, it was over.

With the comforter pulled up around us as we lay in bed, we were still reeling from the events of the evening. We prayed over the home we'd been accused of infecting with darkness; we prayed light, we prayed blessing, we prayed peace.

As we willed ourselves to sleep, we were really just beginning to awaken to life outside of someone else's control.

3

THIRTY DAYS

The one page letter, now crumpled, creased and committed to memory, detailed my indiscretion. I had broken a verbal covenant. It was just one of the reasons for eviction that gave us thirty days to leave.

We were gone in three.

Once we told my family what had happened, they rose to support us and had us packed and moved out by the end of the long weekend following that devastating meeting. We had no place to go. We had never anticipated the kind of rapid relational deterioration that occurred between us and our pastors, friends and landlords.

It was a heart-wrenching pain that sometimes felt sharp and visceral and other times presented itself as a deep, dull, depressing ache. While my family came to our aid physically and emotionally, Veronica's family avoided us completely, eventually rejecting us for the choices we'd made and the journey we'd embarked on.

My siblings appeared the morning after our meeting, ready to assist us in anyway they could. The next day, boxes appeared, a moving truck backed in to the driveway, and before we knew it, they'd helped us pack up our lives and gather our self-respect. I will forever be grateful for the non-judgmental, reassuring support we received that day.

My parents put us up for a few weeks while we searched for a place to call home. The emotional trauma made it difficult to wake up in the morning, let alone dress and feed our girls, get them to school, dress and feed ourselves, and get to work, functioning as productive members of society. We were just going through the motions while we processed the significance of what had occurred. Our faith in leaders, friends, family and God had been shaken. The world as we'd known it had been literally flipped upside down.

Only weeks earlier, our calendar was packed. Monday nights ... leadership meeting. Tuesday morning ... Veronica co-led a women's bible study. Wednesday nights ... midweek service. Nearly every night of the week we would find ourselves at the church, planning for church, or thinking about church. Suddenly, it was over. It was like a bad breakup. We were heartbroken, homeless and without purpose.

We were popular pastors and worship leaders one week, and outcasts the next. Our social media numbers were dropping fast, the same Facebook and Twitter accounts that we once used to promote the ministry's latest conference or event or share Pastor Ken's latest message were now quiet, online reflections of the aloneness we felt. Our calendar went from being jam packed with meetings, services, coffee and dinner dates to an empty collection of little numbered boxes that hung on the kitchen wall next to the fridge.

It felt like we'd been consumed. Chewed up and spit out. Nothing left to give. After all these years of ministry, day in, day out, serving the church, we were now spent. Expired. Worthless. We noticed our social media numbers begin to drop as "friends" still in the church found out what had happened. A few tried to reach out and "save" us, but most just wrote us off and moved on.

That was what we got for giving it our all, planning worship services, organizing band practices, setting up and tearing down week after week. We felt like the kid in the playground that tries to stand up and reason with the bully. You know, the "I'm not asking for any trouble" kid. We may not have been asking for it, but we got it.

Things had gone from great to good to fine to bad to worse in a matter of weeks. Perhaps life meant to make us an example: This is what happens when you question the leadership or challenge the status quo.

We'd bump into people from the church while getting groceries or hanging out at Starbucks, but boy were those conversations awkward! The church leadership had decided that it would be best to let us go quietly, so no real announcement was made except that we were taking a "sabbatical" and would most likely be returning in the fall. This left us with the task of explaining to each individual who asked that we would not be returning.

The ironic part was that the sabbatical was actually what we had hoped for, what we initially requested. The elder board had met and approved our request, extending much grace, love and understanding for our journey. Somewhere between that meeting and the one in which we had just been betrayed, things had gone off the rails.

From the day we left, we didn't receive a single phone call from the friends we'd made at church. Who knows what stories they were told. We heard that some people thought we'd gone on sabbatical. Some had heard we'd "gone organic," which was usually accompanied with a sarcastic or concerned tone, as though we'd gone crazy.

We tried to look to the future, and we tried to understand why this was happening, but for the most part we just survived. This time in our lives was not about answers but questions. And after all the pain had been inflicted and absorbed, more questions remained. There were no answers, and the questions just brought us more pain.

Morning by morning, we settled into some semblance of routine, the shock wearing off. My parents would venture small forays into conversation about our ejection from the church and eviction from our home. We'd answer when we could, but for the most part, we were just hanging on—to each other, to our children, and to whatever dignity remained.

We were broken. Putting the pieces back together meant understanding why. I've once heard it put this way: "If you want to know where you're going, look back at where you came from." In an attempt to discover how we'd gotten ourselves emotionally and spiritually train wrecked, and how we'd be able to recover, we'd have to look back at where we'd been.

4

PUTTING DOWN ROOTS

I met my wife, Veronica, in the nursery room at our church, so you could literally say we grew up in the church. Since our parents had put us both in the same church-run private school, we spent more time growing up together in that place than we spent apart from each other in our separate homes.

Veronica and I often spoke of life "in the bubble," since our church, home and school experiences were all blended together. We were well protected from the dangers of life. I remember thinking early on that public school must be a very dirty, sinful and scary place. There were rumors that the kids out there in the public schools didn't even wear uniforms. I couldn't imagine the chaos. I enjoyed being a part of our tribe: two hundred and thirty-six white-shirt, blue-pants, and maroon-sweater-wearing kindergarten to grade twelve students.

I made my first attempt at wooing Veronica in the fourth grade, as we found ourselves together in the same tire swing, with each of our legs through the middle of the tire, our outside shoes churning up the pea gravel as we spun like mad until the other kids hanging on flew off. From that day on I was "in love." I just knew I would marry her, or at least I hoped I could win her heart.

I finally worked up the courage to ask her to the school's Christmas banquet when I was fourteen and she was sixteen. We were standing next to the school's only vending machine, and I was keeping it cool and casual until suddenly I heard these words as they fell clumsily out of my mouth: "So I was wondering, do you think you could or would, ahem, go to the banquet with me?" I asked with all the strength and vigor of a nervous kitten, my voice cracking as I delivered my request.

"Go with you to the banquet!?" she asked, with an incredulous look in her eyes. "You're not even old enough to drive!" I nearly died. I had expected a much simpler, less flamboyant response. Quite the crowd of onlookers had gathered, and this was a significant blow to my confidence.

After regaining my courage I asked her again, this time clarifying the question, asking if she would sit with me at the banquet. To my great joy and relief, she agreed. I cemented my resolve then and there to marry her, as I would never be able to muster up the courage to ask anything of another girl ever again.

In our teenage years, we added youth group to the mix of our activities, and though we were still blending with the same group of kids we'd grown up at school and church with, this was where we first felt like we were gaining our independence.

On the first Thursday night after my fourteenth birthday, my mom dropped me off at the youth leader's home at quarter to seven. It was my first time there; I'd avoided it while I was thirteen for some reason, but at fourteen, my parents felt it was time I go. One of the youth leaders had heard I could play piano. He had arranged to have a keyboard set up and told me we'd be leading worship together.

So, from the first time I'd been brave enough to attend youth group, I was standing at the front, learning to play the classics like Hillsong's Shout to the Lord and Delirious' I Found Jesus. Even better, I was learning to do it in style, on a Yamaha PSR-250 electric keyboard with a drum machine that someone had borrowed from his grandmother. I only used the drum machine once, until the laughter of my audience helped me learn never to press that bright yellow button marked Rhythm Accompaniment ever again.

I still remember the very first song we played on my very first Thursday night. It was a song I'd never heard before, "Come and Fill Me Up" by Brian Doerksen. The lead sheet I was handed moments before we played had chords written in the key of A, but a few were scribbled out and replaced with chords in the key of G. Since I was a worship-leading rookie, I had yet to discover that this was a very common practice amongst amateur worship leading musicians, especially the guitar playing ones...I think because they have something against the F sharp minor (F#m) chord.

Needless to say, I was nervous. This was my first time playing worship songs, in front of a group of fifty people, many of whom I knew from church and school. The guy leading worship looked over at me and said, "Oh yeah, we're playing that one in G. You can transpose on the fly, right?"

"Uh, yeah, of course," I lied, hoping the confidence in my voice would mask the musical mess I was about to create.

Needless to say, it was a rough start, but we got there. Three fast songs, one with an emotion-evoking key change mid-song, followed by two slow songs, and my part of the evening was done. From that night on, at youth, school chapel or church, I would be found at the front or on stage, playing my heart out and singing to Jesus.

I'd found a place of belonging, a place I could call my own. I was mediocre as a basketball player, a "B" average student and by no means one of the popular kids. Standing behind my keyboard with my eyes glued shut, singing worship songs, gave me meaning and purpose.

The presence of God became a place of solace and rest for me. I was confident, secure and at peace. I could get lost there.

There's something about making music and singing together that inspires me and warms my heart to this very day. Even though in the years to come we'd discover how worship is judged, criticized, used and abused, there is still a spark in my heart that longs to hear the pure, sacred sound played by artists unadulterated by the agenda of a praise and worship service. For me, there is nothing more worshipful than that.

Eventually, Veronica joined me as a worship leader, and we led worship together for the next fifteen years. We even led worship at our wedding! We married in the summer after high school (it was either marry early or "burn with passion," as they say), surrounded by friends and family from our church, school and youth group.

From our wedding day forward, we journeyed through life mixing our personal life with church, ministry and leadership issues. Together, we were impressionable and perhaps a little naïve, but we we were such open books, open to input, encouragement and the discipline of our parents, elders and church leaders. We didn't realize we were allowing the roots of our lives to grow together, so entwined with the thoughts, morals and theological beliefs of others we weren't thinking for ourselves.

During our wedding ceremony, we had asked all of the spiritual leaders in our lives to gather and pray for us. We were so honored to have at least ten locally prominent ministry personalities in attendance, their lengthy prayers and prophetic words adding nearly thirty minutes to the festivities. There was even a spontaneous song. It may have seemed foreign to some of the wedding guests, but kneeling together amongst this collective of ministers, we felt like we were right where we belonged.

Looking back, the image of these pastors and their wives gathered around this young, talented, vibrant couple is a good way to describe the true picture of our venture into the world as a couple. I can't help but feel as though when each of them prayed over us they were laying claim to our future in ministry. We were beginning our own, independent life together, but we were bringing along the opinions, thoughts, feelings and emotions of many church leaders.

As our life together was just beginning, the roots we were putting down were already becoming twisted into the ground with those who were gathered to pray for us. At the time, we felt blessed to be loved by so many important people; it felt like we were being drawn into the fold.

5

FOLLOW ME, LET'S START A MINISTRY

Shortly after our wedding day, Veronica and I connected with Ken and Diane, a missionary couple based in Mexico whom our church and my family had supported over the years. Home from the mission field on a brief furlough, we had been honored by their attendance at our wedding as we really admired them as ministers of the gospel. They were beloved by most of the people who attended the church we'd been raised in.

These were the people who were actually "doing the stuff" we believed in. These were the people who would come home once or twice per year from their base in Mexico and present to our church the amazing results of the ministry they had been engaged in.

Ken and Diane were one of the couples that had gathered around us to pray on our wedding day. The words he spoke in front of the hundred and thirty gathered guests became one of the primary topics of conversation for Veronica and me on our honeymoon.

He prophesied that we would travel and minister together in the future, and that we were part of a royal priesthood that was not of the world. He spoke with such confidence of a future where Veronica and I would be in relationship with him and Diane. The words he gave at our wedding would become the path on which we travelled as a married couple, self-fulfilling the prophecy he gave that day.

Ken seemed more enthusiastic about ministry than any spiritual leader I'd ever met and he seemed to see a lot of potential in me. Each time Veronica and I would join their family for dinner, we would leave encouraged. Ken would consistently call out the potential for greatness he could see in me and in us as a team.

Only months after marrying, Veronica and I began planning to lead our first short-term missions trip as a couple. I was only nineteen years old at the time, but I put out the word that we'd be leading a missions trip to do music and drama ministry in San Jose del Cabo and La Paz, Mexico. I made a point to announce that we would be ministering in conjunction with Ken and Diane, our church's favorite missionaries. Before we knew it, we had a team.

There were literally hundreds of emails exchanged between Ken and me during the four-month planning stage of this missions trip. Ken obsessed over the most tedious of details, and I learned to operate in a similar manner. I didn't really notice that he was hovering over the smallest issues, but Veronica sure did. From the very beginning, Veronica could see the control at work.

As we were preparing for the trip, Ken sent an extremely detailed dress code for the women on our team. In addition to specifically banning bikinis and the exposure of cleavage or midriff, his modesty manifesto was comprehensive, covering every last detail. It even included the appropriate number of inches wide (2") for a tank top strap to be. We weren't new to restrictive dress codes, growing up in the same church/school that we would be travelling under the auspices of.

There was literally no mention of a dress code for the men.

Personally, I didn't feel slighted, but looking back I am certain I downplayed Veronica's opinion of the matter, in the name of spiritual submission. In my desire to gain his favor, I began to elevate his voice over hers.

We continued to prepare for the first mission's trip on which we'd be considered the leaders. Ken even recommended that we get a base tan before heading south, to minimize the risk of sunburn. Born and raised in a suburb of Vancouver, BC, Canada, we don't really have an option to tan naturally in February and March (or most other months—in case you aren't familiar with our corner of the globe, we get a lot of rain).

Months of "Mexico Meetings" (our weekly, two hour planning and rehearsal times) later, we departed, tanned and ready for our missions trip.

We arrived in San Jose del Cabo late on a Friday afternoon in March, and I remember disembarking from the plane and being hit with the hot, humid smells of Mexico. I squinted while walking down the stairs and onto the glimmering tarmac, confident that adventure awaited.

Ken became one of my personal heroes on that trip as we went from church to church, sharing our heavily-accented, poorly-translated worship songs. Being a young leader, I faced some challenges with members of our team ranging in age from 17-45, but when any of them questioned a decision I made, Ken backed me up, empowering and defending me.

On one of our first nights, we had gathered behind the huge yellow circus tent we would be ministering in that evening. We were planning out our set of music and organizing the order of service. A couple of the team members felt I wasn't qualified to decide which song to play when or who to tap to deliver their testimony.

These team members, who were about the same age as my parents and were experienced leaders back home, took their complaint to Ken. I listened to their exchange through the thin vinyl wall of the circus tent. He became furious with them for questioning my judgment. He insisted they submit to the authority he had given to me.

As I graciously accepted the apology of my insubordinate team members, I was swelling with pride. In that moment I learned to trust Ken unconditionally. I felt great worth because of the way he validated me and affirmed my leadership.

Ken taught me how to lead people and spoke of grooming me for future ministry.

We talked a lot about my need for spiritual covering on that trip. He put it out there that he considered me a spiritual son. I didn't really know what that meant at the time, but it made me feel important when he said it.

I stayed close to Ken for the entire trip, shadowing his every move. I observed as he bribed the Mexican police who'd pulled us over for riding in the back of the pickup and sat close to the front when he preached, ready to jump up and play music as he closed his message.

He and I developed a special hand signal on that trip that we'd use until the very last time I'd lead worship for him, well over ten years later. When he wanted a little music to undergird the finale of his sermon, he'd make eye contact with me and drum his fingers on the pulpit or against his leg, signaling that it was time for me to make my way to the piano, and together we'd knock the service out of the park.

On one of our two days off while serving in Mexico, we went to the beach as a team. Ken didn't really like resting or playing and was going to spend the afternoon in the shade, working on his computer. I did the same. Ever since he called me his spiritual son, I felt this deep need to serve him and his vision. Veronica stood at the water's edge, dressed in compliance with the ministry's one-piece swimsuit rule, and playfully beckoned me to into the ocean, wanting me to play in the surf with her and the rest of the team. I smiled, but chose to stay with Ken on the shore, deciding it was more important to help him wherever I could.

She shrugged and smiled back, giving me sort of a "you're missing all the fun" look, and bounced back into the teal water.

This is just one small example of the many times I chose my mentor over my wife and lover. Like me, Veronica understood the importance of spiritual covering, leadership and all of the related religious stuff; it had been hammered into us since shortly after meeting one another as toddlers. As my newlywed bride frolicked in the waves, trying desperately to draw my attention, I focused on what I assumed were more important things, kingdom things.

Spending time with Ken made me feel needed, important and valued. I felt "called." He shared with me his vision to create a ministry organization that would be independent of his current affiliation with the church we were both members of back in Canada. He talked of the poverty mentality surrounding church-sponsored missionaries and how they were barely making it financially.

He inspired me to give more of our own money to support him and Diane as they thanklessly toiled together in Mexico. He spoke of a bright future where we would have an opportunity to literally change the world.

I listened to his vision of creating his own worldwide missions organization and felt like I'd found where I was meant to be. He told me the name he had come up with for the new ministry but insisted I keep it secret until he returned to Canada. As he spoke, I felt even more honored than I already did because he was trusting me with his plans for the future—plans that didn't necessarily line up with the direction of the leadership of our church back in Canada.

Ken didn't seem to get all wrapped up in the red tape of ministry. Where there was a need, he filled it. He didn't try, he didn't like to consult with boards. He just did what needed to be done. I was inspired to grow closer to this groundbreaking missionary renegade.

Veronica, however, was frustrated. "He doesn't even talk to me," she'd say. "He doesn't even look me in the eye." It's true. He didn't. Ministry was a male-dominated field, and his wife, Diane, was very submissive and very much in the background. Veronica also noticed how stressed and on edge I was while near Pastor Ken, making it feel like she couldn't enjoy herself. I said and did things that were out of character for me and that made her feel like she was less important than my new ministry idol.

Ken would make vague implications about how a leader and his wife should conduct themselves but would usually stop short of telling me to better control my wife. He would often point to Diane as a shining example of how a wife should behave, speak and dress in ministry.

On more than one occasion I worked up the courage to criticize Veronica's outfit for not being modest enough for a woman in ministry or her behavior for being less than befitting of a leader's wife. These views weren't really my own, but I was doing my best to do and say what I thought Ken would want me to do and say. Most of the time he wouldn't come right out and criticize her appearance, but his "advice' would come disguised within some kind of compliment.

"She's a beautiful woman, Travis," he'd begin before going on to explain why she'd have to learn to dress more conservatively, walk less provocatively. And, as a good "son," I would relay his concerns, delivering his words as though they were my own.

As a person with a charismatic, engaging personality, Veronica felt like she had to compete for my attention while we were in the presence of this charismatic, engaging leader. She was conflicted. She was jealous that she had to share me with Ken on our first big missions trip but also proud that I seemed to receive such honor from him, even though she didn't really understand why I was getting so much attention.

The only time Veronica and I spent away from Ken and the rest of our team was at night after the evening church services we were leading. On one of the final nights of the missions trip, in the cottage reserved for married couples at the edge of the compound, it came out. Veronica started by complaining to me about her feelings and her fear that I was being controlled by Ken.

"You're captivated by him. You don't even see me," she said, frustrated. "I'm a young and beautiful woman, on a beach in Mexico!"

"This isn't a vacation, Veronica," I began, taking on a tone of voice that suggested more of a parent/child relationship than that of a marriage partner. "This is about the Lord's work. We must remember that we are here to serve." At the time, believing I was her spiritual covering, I was doing my best to live up to my God-given calling as a new husband.

Though I responded defensively and couldn't admit it at the time, her words were true. I was captivated by Ken. He had an ability to inspire, to cause his followers to feel an increased self worth and confidence. He was able to wield this power by revealing greatness in the people around him and then "plugging them in" to various areas of service within the ministry. He was larger than life, and when he spoke, he captivated his audience. He seemed to have an extra measure of power that no one else had.

Veronica hated that Ken had this power and used it to wield control over me and thus over her. Veronica's father was very controlling over her as a child, and, as an independent woman married to a strong man, she never expected to be controlled again in her life. On our wedding night, she thanked me for saving her from the controlling grasp of her father.

"You're spending all your time with him! I'm your wife, Travis. Look at me! What is more important? Me or ministry?" she cried as she released her feelings of jealousy, pain and inadequacy.

We'd only been married for about six months, but the tension was pulling us apart. We were still just learning how to live together, and, in the beginning, sex was quite painful for Veronica. We'd both waited for marriage but quickly discovered that the blessed sex we'd been promised for remaining pure until our wedding day wasn't going to come easily.

From our honeymoon onward, we'd experienced about three months of bad sex, sex that caused Veronica pain and me frustration, and then we just stopped having sex for the next three months.

Looking back, I can see that Veronica was trying to attract me, to entice me. There we were in a beautiful locale, my beautiful bride was trying to catch my attention, but because I assumed we wouldn't be consummating our love, I wasn't even noticing her. And what made matters worse, I'd found something more important on which to turn my attention.

Veronica could see how much time and love I had for Ken, and she viewed him not only as competition for my time and attention but also for my emotional energy.

She stood by the light switch, naked, and sobbed, "I have nothing to offer you that he can't! If my beauty doesn't entice you, and I can't give you my body, then what?!"

She turned out the lights and came to bed. Instead of turning away from each other, we turned in. We made love for the first time in nearly three months, and I could feel the tears continue to stream down her face as we did. On that very night, she would later tell me, she resolved to become more submissive and quiet about her own emotional needs in order to save our marriage.

She did this because she came to the realization that she would have to share me and my attentions with Ken. I hated having to choose between Veronica and Ken, but Ken had inspired me, and I was convinced that following him would be the best thing for both Veronica and me.

The trip ended, and though we returned home to Canada, Ken and I continued to correspond back and forth until he returned to Canada in the fall of 2003. After church one Sunday, Ken approached me outside in the parking lot.

"It's time," he said. "I'm going to be launching my new para-Church ministry." He was referring to the vision for a missions organization he'd first shared with me months earlier in Mexico. "I want you to be one of the founding board members. It's an opportunity to get in on the ground floor," he continued.

I had fallen head over heels for the vision he had shared with me months earlier down in Mexico as we'd looked over the sea of Cortez and watched my team frolic in the waves. They'd been blissfully ignorant of the important, world-changing conversations we were having in the shade.

All of the dreams he had inspired in me back then were about to become true. As we conversed out behind the church, we spoke in semi-hushed tones, knowing that the institution on whose gravel parking lot we stood wouldn't approve of our creation of a para-church ministry, especially one that wasn't under its covering.

I felt the way a disciple must have felt being called by Jesus but also a little like a rebellious teenager, planning to pull a fast one on my spiritual parents. I'd been born into and raised in this church, a church in which Ken served on the leadership. And yet, we were keeping our plans secret from that same leadership team. It was a recipe that caused my pride to soar, and being as young as I was, I wasn't really thinking about what it is that pride is said to precede.

6

ANGELS AMONG US

All of my available time over the next couple of years was spent doing the legwork to launch our new ministry. Filing applications, creating logos and ministry brochures, receiving the mail, sending out donor support letters, maintaining the website, doing bank deposits, and all of the other administrative work that comes with running a non-profit organization. Everything I did was as a volunteer. All of the donations we received were used to fund Ken and Diane and their ministry work.

We served their vision tirelessly, providing as much support as we could, both with our time and our money. At the time, we truly felt like we were launching something amazing from the ground up, something that could change the world. We knew Ken and Diane were out there doing good work, but we always looked forward to their return. We'd grown to rely on them to "pour into us" and inspire us.

Anytime they came home from the "field," we cleared our schedules and made ourselves available to serve in any way we could.

On one such occasion, they'd returned home from Mexico for two weeks over Christmas and had invited us for dinner in Diane's parents home, where they were staying. Veronica and I had now been married for just about four years.

They welcomed us into the family home as though it was their own. Diane had made a delicious dinner, and she and Veronica were clearing the table while "the men" (Ken and I) headed into the living room with our pie and ice cream.

Ken had a way of inspiring anyone as well as engaging their service and support. I remember taking a big mouthful of Diane's warm berry crumble when he began speaking of the future of the ministry. He wasn't just dreaming for the next year or even the next decade; he began talking about who would take the reins after him. And he was looking at me.

"You'll be the president of the ministry when it's time for me to retire," he said. I was speechless. Though I am a visionary, his grasp on the future far outreached mine.

I was hooked. Though we weren't a big organization yet, by any stretch of the imagination, the potential was there. And it would all be mine someday.

Ken considered himself a prophet, and not just any prophet. He was a "see-er" prophet; at least, that is what he told us. Ken believed he could "see" into the spiritual realm that was "all around us."

We used to hold our semiannual board meetings in a local diner. After one of our earliest meetings, over decaf coffee and banana crème pie, we made our way out to the parking lot, and, as was usually the case, Ken was still talking about what he could "see."

My dad, who was also a board member, asked Ken curiously, "So you can see into the supernatural, right now?"

"Yes," he said, looking off into the distance, waiting for the follow up question.

"Well, what do you see right now?" asked my Dad excitedly, his curiosity getting the best of him. Normally my Dad was pretty levelheaded about this kind of thing, but when someone he trusted could see into the spiritual realm, he wanted to hear all about it.

Wouldn't you know it, at the very same moment my Dad asked the question, we just happened to be standing in the presence of a very powerful supernatural being.

"Over there, standing on the sign for the Best Western hotel, is an angel looking over this way." Ken went on, "He's a big one, probably standing ten or twelve feet high. He's a warrior angel."

Ken went on to explain what it meant to have this particular angel nearby. There were great things in store for us, and this angel had been sent to protect the plan of God for our bourgeoning ministry. Angels sent to protect our vision? As I said, Ken had a way of making anyone feel like they were a valued part of the most amazing opportunity.

Standing in the parking lot on that cold Monday night in September, we were all amazed. Well, most of us. It's not that I didn't want to believe. I felt like a kid who knew his parents delivered the Christmas presents but still wanted desperately to believe in Santa Claus. I wanted nothing more than to believe. I was fine with it all as long as Ken was there to explain his visions. Whenever someone questioned me as to the validity of his claims, I would grow incredibly squeamish.

This wasn't the only time angels would be a topic of conversation.

~

Ken and Diane and their family spent most of the their time on the mission field in Mexico, but they also travelled throughout the United States and Canada on our behalf in partnership with a very prominent, charismatic, I'll-pray-for-you-and-you'll-fall-on-the-floor kind of "signs and wonders" ministry.

Ken had begun working with the "signs and wonders" crowd after our ministries crossed paths in our hometown.

Theirs was the kind of ministry that regularly reported angel feathers wafting from heaven during worship or supernatural gold dust appearing on the faces of ministers as they spoke. They also claimed "dental" miracles, fillings appearing in the mouths of worshippers that were "better than any dentist could have made."

Personally, I was never comfortable with this kind of ministry. I wanted Ken to stay as far away from that stuff as possible. Even though they were often the subjects of scandal, Ken felt like he could incrementally increase our reach by partnering with this high profile group.

Even after the maintenance staff of a conference venue confirmed that the "angel feathers" falling during a worship service were actually the feathers of molting pigeons that had made a nest in the air conditioning ducts, Ken still felt it important to remain connected.

Searching for little gems from heaven on the carpet beneath my pew, listening to gold dust-covered preachers, or getting my dental work done by God wasn't what my faith in Jesus was all about. I stuck with Ken, however, as I trusted him blindly. If he thought it was a good thing, then that was good enough for me.

Since Ken had begun referring to me as his "spiritual son" all those years earlier in Mexico, I felt indebted to him for the honor. I would often make myself available to drive him to or from the airport at any hour of the day or night, even though I worked a full-time job. I wanted to serve him in any way I could.

On one such late night pick up, upon returning from Mexico, Ken could hardly contain his excitement when he got in the van. "We've got angel pictures," he said, beaming from ear to ear. I really didn't even know where to go with that one.

He couldn't help himself. We pulled into a parking lot and he booted up his seventeen-inch HP laptop. He was obsessed with having the biggest and best. It was even written into the ministry's constitution that we'd use whatever technological means possible to win the lost.

As the Windows XP operating system loaded, he explained what had happened on his latest ministry trip to the southern Baja with a well-known travelling minister. Our ministry had been hosting this prominent international ministry and its famous healing evangelist for a series of evangelistic crusades. For one of the evenings we'd rented a small stadium, and thousands of people had come to be touched by God or at least fall over under his power. God was knocking a lot of people to the ground in our particular stream of ministry during that particular time.

Ken explained that he had been taking pictures of the people in attendance at the crusade and while reviewing them afterwards noticed something "amazing." He turned the laptop so I could see the screen.

"Do you see them?" he asked, excitedly. "Orbs!" He could hardly contain his excitement. I'd never heard of an "orb" before. Fortunately, he was able to explain it as some paranormal, supernatural phenomenon.

He continued to scroll through the photos, pointing out not only the orbs but other large, shadowed "figures" in the darkened arena: more "warrior angels." Finally, in an image someone had taken of him, Ken asked me to increase the contrast in the dark area of the photo above his left shoulder. I complied, and he rejoiced.

"You see?" he exclaimed, "A 'messenger' angel! Right there, above my shoulder!"

I didn't ask how he knew what type of angel it was. To me it looked more like the shadows of an indoor plant near the back of the stage. He was so thrilled with himself. He was more excited about this than I'd ever seen him.

Months later, when I'd finally let my skepticism get the best of me, I searched out what causes "orbs" in digital photography. It turns out, there is a scientific explanation for the phenomenon of the "orbs"—not that any of us really trusted science. Faith was what mattered. If ever a conflict arose that pitted that which we believed with that which was scientifically proven, faith would win every time. Even when I took him the information I gleaned about what caused the orbs in his photos, that they were appearing as a result of light reflecting off dust, he still chose to believe.

I wanted to get caught up in the excitement; I wanted to believe. In fact, I actually had to believe. I felt like if I didn't believe, I would lose my place as his right hand man, his "son." I had been making a habit of pushing down my doubts and fears the moment they became apparent. I prayed to God to take away my doubts, to help my unbelief. I adopted a "fake it 'til you make it" strategy. This was Ken's power over me. I didn't want to lose my place of honor. I allowed the control in exchange for a position of power.

Whenever I felt like challenging my mentor I would instead renew my trust in him.

"We're going to release an interactive CD-ROM of these pictures for ten dollars a disc," he declared. "We've got our first product!"

I was skeptical, but I submitted. It was the first time I'd heard the word "product" associated with ministry, but it would hardly be the last. Every ministry in the signs and wonders crowd travelled with truckloads of material to sell at conferences and events. Carrying product made both of us feel like we were becoming a legitimate ministry.

Somehow I was able reconcile the fact that we were creating a business out of our non-profit organization, simply because everyone who was anyone was doing it. I didn't feel that selling product to raise funds for missions work or ministry was inherently wrong, but the way we talked about it, the way we went about it, left a bad taste in my mouth.

After their release, we would often receive extremely negative criticism regarding the angel CDs. People posted negative remarks online against our ministry, trying to prove that our claim of capturing photographs of angels was false. We prayed against this persecution for the obvious attack from the evil one that we believed it was. Those who criticized the ministry were seen as spiritual attacks rather than people who could see through the smoke screen.

Over the next several years, we became quite wrapped up in the ministry we had created. While Ken continued to travel and minister with various big name healing evangelists, Veronica and I formed a worship band that travelled and ministered under the banner of our newly-formed ministry. Veronica, myself and five others played over one hundred and fifty worship services during the three years we were active as a worship band.

With this band, we led a second mission's trip to Mexico, this time learning songs that were actually sung in the churches we visited. While in the country, our team of musicians/carpenters also built an addition onto a church.

It was on this trip that I really got sold on the potential good we could do as a ministry. Once again, we met up with Ken in San Jose del Cabo and this time in addition to the musical instruments we carried, we also packed three large cases of construction equipment.

We travelled in a three-vehicle convoy into the desert, driving for nearly twelve hours before reaching our destination, which was only one hundred kilometers away. We could have almost walked faster. The road was one of the worst I've ever driven, through forests of cacti and across small rocky rivers. As night fell, we crested a small mountain and carefully drove the tight switchbacks down in the valley below into a small fishing village known as Los Burros.

It was in this village that we ministered for five days, performing a major renovation to the tiny church building by day and performing worship music by night. It was an amazing experience.

Veronica was probably the only one who really didn't enjoy herself there, as Ken felt it necessary to inform her that being the only woman travelling with this many guys would look bad to the local villagers.

In addition, Ken insisted that while we ministered in this village she must wear long skirts or pants, long sleeve shirts and closed-toe shoes so as not to appear immodest to the locals.

To put it mildly, this dress code was overkill. Most of the local women were dressed much more comfortably than Veronica, who now seemed quite awkward and out of place. Not only that, she felt shame about her body due the warning Ken had given her about the potential for her to cause one of these innocent fisherman to stumble by lusting after her.

Unfortunately, I did nothing to defend my wife from this discriminating body shaming. I took Ken's word as gospel and insisted that she comply with whatever rules he imposed. And so, while keeping Veronica safely hidden away from view inside the church, we continued to do our work.

It was just another slight against Veronica. She was used to being less important, she was used to submitting. We'd both been raised with the understanding that women are to submit to their husbands and church leaders. There was no room for her to stand up for herself, and I surely wasn't sticking my neck out for her. What Ken said was pretty much what God would say as far as I was concerned.

By some miracle, Veronica and I did enjoy one memory of freedom-inspiring insubordination while we ministered in Los Burros. There was a small swimming hole near the mountain that our team snuck off to enjoy during the hottest part of the day on one of our last days in the village. It was so beautiful and secluded. We enjoyed our swim and were preparing to head back when one of my best friends took me aside and said he and a couple of the band members would be happy to stand guard a minute or so down the path if Veronica and I would like to enjoy the natural beauty of this special place alone.

He didn't have to ask twice. Veronica didn't even wait until they were out of earshot to peel off the one-piece swimsuit she had been required to purchase to protect her modesty. As the Lycra suit landed against the rocks, her beauty captured my attention. In that moment, nothing about the ministry mattered. Two lovers reunited in the luscious landscape, lost in love while time stood still.

This tiny taste of freedom from the nodding-headed yes man I had become made me want to run away and never come back. My attention had been directed back to Veronica in an undivided way for that short window of time. It made me miss a simpler life together.

As she stood naked before me and God in that Mexican oasis, I truly saw her. Before that moment I don't think I'd even really looked at her since before we boarded the plane back in Canada.

Veronica had been so submitted to the idea I was slowly dedicating my life to serve Ken that I'd forgotten how electric we were as a couple. She had become a third wheel to the dynamic ministry duo that Ken and I were growing into.

Though this moment was forgotten as soon as Ken recaptured my attention back at camp, an indelible mark was left on my heart. I would seek to find this feeling of freedom again in the future, though I wouldn't know what I was looking for.

The sun was beginning to set, so we dressed and headed down the path. My friend who'd suggested the rendezvous and two other bandmates waited about a minute's walk away from the secluded spot carved into the mountain. They all smiled at me knowingly, and I smiled back while Veronica smiled but looked away. None of us spoke of this to Pastor Ken, as we were pretty sure the missionary's position on skinny-dipping and sex in the outdoors wouldn't be a favorable one.

Even though we didn't speak of our jungle rendezvous to Ken, it was almost like he sensed a refreshed connection between Veronica and me. He acted jealous whenever my wife and I seemed close. That very night we rode with the team in the box of his pickup to the beach for some stargazing. Though typically a romantic event for lovers, on this occasion Ken beckoned me to the waters edge.

I left Veronica standing near the truck with the rest of the team and walked toward where the water lapped at the sand. As I approached and knelt next to him, he reached into the water, withdrawing a white shell.

"Someday, I'll walk on water…literally," he said, his voice taking on a prophetic tone. He passed the shell to me as he continued, "This shell will represent God's promise to me that I will someday walk on the water like Jesus did."

As my mentor, idol and hero, I believed him. I believed in him.

When I handed the shell back to Ken, he broke it in half. He threw one half back into the water and tucked the other half in his pocket. He explained it was a prophetic act that someday God would honor his promise.

Part of me just wanted to tell him to do it. Right then and there. Walk on the water. But I knew it didn't work that way. I would just have to have to wait and have faith.

We walked back to the truck, to the rest of the team and a very jealous Veronica, a jealousy that had transferred from Ken to her in a matter of minutes.

On the last day before leaving this remote village, several fishermen approached us about a need in the community. Chofee, a fisherman who also led the church, had a problem. The outboard engine on his small fishing boat had died. One of the guys on our team was a mechanic and took a look at it. To his chagrin, it had probably been repaired time and again with whatever shoestring or coat hanger they could find and he confirmed the motor was done.

Without a working fishing boat, Chofee was left with no way to make a living and would have to leave the village in search of work and a way to support his family. This would also leave the church we'd just renovated, a project that doubled its size, without the man who had led it since it's inception.

Our team gathered together and considered our options. We sat in a circle in the sand in the shade of our dirty, white four-wheel drive fifteen passenger van. We'd all brought enough money to enjoy ourselves on this trip, to eat well and buy souvenirs. One of the band members suddenly spoke up and offered $800 of his own money. Then another. Another gave $565, which was all the money he had with him, but would send more once we got back to town. One by one, each person chipped in, out of our own pockets, and right then and there our team of ten had raised the $6500 needed for a new engine and other repairs to Chofee's boat.

It was an amazing experience and a memory I will never forget. We were living out what the Church is really all about. We were followers of Jesus making a difference in the world, a tangible, physical difference in people's lives. This is where I started to develop a "this is church" attitude as I witnessed a sensory, organic connection between God and man.

Even though in my heart I was struggling with the level of control imposed specifically on Veronica and women in ministry in general, there was so much good being done. It was this tension that allowed me to turn a blind eye to certain issues. Who was I to question the status quo when God was moving in such tangible ways?

We were witnessing the kingdom of heaven revealed on earth which had everything to do with the generous love of God being shared through people loving people and nothing to do with a non-profit ministry selling retouched photos of angels and orbs for $10 apiece. I chose to overlook one in order to continue to experience the other.

7

MISSIONS PORN AND STUDIO TIME

In the first two years of having a bona-fide non-profit organization, we exhibited our ministry at an annual event showcasing the latest and greatest missions organizations, from sponsor-a-child organizations to drinking well drillers to Christian children's camps to English as a second language groups.

Everyone had a CD or a T-shirt or a monthly-sponsorship form or a brochure or a pen or a notepad or a knick-knack from some developing country. We weren't supposed to sell anything, as all sales had to be run through the official festival store so they could take their cut. Nonetheless, there definitely was a black-market, under-the-table economy in play, and you could buy our angel pic CDs from us for ten bucks. Cash.

It hurts my heart to think back to the plastic bags covered in the flashy branding of a local Christian radio station, filled with moneymaking missions propaganda. I was forced to realize, from first-hand experience, the industry that missions and non-profit work had become. If there was ever a place where I could see Jesus flipping over tables, it was here.

More, more, more. It was all about getting more. Not more souls for Christ. Not more of God in our lives. It was about more money. That's why we were there, after all, claiming our eight feet by four feet section of plush blue carpet, against a blue and gold pipe and drape background, in front of a six foot table rented from the festival for twenty-five dollars, with our laptops plugged into an electrical outlet, also rented from the festival (sixty-five dollars), while seated on two folding chairs (at ten dollars each).

In addition to all of that, we commissioned the creation of a custom banner to showcase our ministry which featured our ministry name, our flashy logo and our slogan superimposed over faces of ten little Mexican children to represent our vision for the world. Not that we had any thing to do with child rescue or orphanages...yet. We'd do whatever God called us to do—or whatever people would pledge money towards.

Looking back, it was ministry-porn at it's finest, each organization flaunting its assets and vying for the same donor dollar. All that was missing were strobe lights and a pole. We were right there in the middle of it, pretty much stepping into the walking paths of potential ministry partners and drawing them into our thirty-two square foot booth to brag about the good we were doing in the world and explain how they would receive a greater reward if they would join us on our mission to change the world.

I wish I could say that during all of this I was being held against my will, forced at gunpoint to parrot the ministry's party line and hawk our product. But the truth is, I was all in. I'd bought Ken's vision, and as Secretary-Treasurer of our newly-minted, federally recognized charity, I was financially responsible for it as well.

I was definitely caught up in it all, although I was deeply conflicted. I returned home to Veronica after each day of the three-day event and confessed my misgivings, my doubts and my tension with the format. I'm sure much good comes from events like this, but I was only really experiencing the seedier side of things, the cynicism, and the jaded double-talk from the mouths of people who claimed to be ministers of the gospel.

One thing was for sure, I didn't ever want to become like them.

Looking around, the room at all of the ministries represented, Ken told me of their high administration costs and about how little of the money raised in events like these actually made it "to the ground." I knew there was so much good we could do in the world, but more importantly, I knew we could do it better and more efficiently than most of the ministries we were "competing" with at that year's missions festival. I really didn't know why we were there. As far as

I could tell, it was just what non-profit organizations did. I had a hard time personally reconciling our promotional actions as a collective with the mission and message of Jesus.

Recalling the atmosphere of the festival causes me to get a bad taste in my mouth. All of these people, leaders in ministry and pastors of churches, all out bragging about the good they were doing in the world, trying to entice people to join, partner, team up and GIVE! I can't think of any other "Christian" event that is more self-seeking than these missions exhibitions were.

If everyone in the room, and I include myself without qualification; if everyone who was responsible for exhibiting and spending thousands of dollars in booth space, booth accessories, marketing materials and wages (yes, many of the people exhibiting were paid, via donor funds, to be there), had instead stayed home and read Jesus' Sermon on the Mount then the world would have become a better place, if even for a day.

I have to clarify, we weren't being evil. We just got caught up in a toxic ministry-culture that is simply counter to the culture of the Kingdom of heaven that Jesus teaches us about in Matthew 5. All we wanted to do was minister; it didn't matter where or how.

We'd literally ask anyone we could reel into our booth what their vision was, and we'd try to convince them that partnering with us could potentially lead to seeing their vision fulfilled. It didn't feel like we were lying. We would simply reveal our honest interest in people's vision for ministry and find a way to make them believe we were the best vehicle to help achieve their goals.

"Orphanages?" Yeah, we could do that.

"Short-term missions?" Sure. Where would you like to go?

If you were able to raise the funds, we'd be more than willing to "cover" your vision for a small administration fee. That's what we were all about, covering and empowering people. Covering was very important to us back then, and it still is to many leaders in the evangelical movement. It was all about submission, being under an umbrella. It basically comes down to control. The more you cover, the more you control.

We'd offer you a legitimate platform from which to minister and in turn add another type of ministry to promote from our website. We wanted to grow and expand. It was more about being important than it was about money. Power is a very real currency in the ministry world.

~

Through it all, I got to thinking about my own vision for ministry, and I imagined how I would like to be empowered. As a worship leader and a songwriter, I dreamt of recording our own album. Shortly after seeing how open we were to people's ministry visions, I pitched the idea to Ken and the rest of our board.

"Record your own worship album?" Go for it! If you can raise the funds, you can do it.

And so, in the fall and winter of 2005, we saved a lot of our own money and raised funds from family and friends, finally booking studio time in November. There we were, recording our own album, under the covering of our ministry.

I chose the month of November to book recording time because I knew Ken would be away ministering and wouldn't be able to interfere with our vision for the album. A former rocker now in his late forties, he'd played guitar with some local bands in the seventies and was very interested in the music we made.

Ken had even played with our band for about six months about a year prior, after he and Diane and their family relocated from the mission field, choosing to base their ministry from here in Canada. He had convinced me that he should be a part of our ministry's band now that he was based locally. Having him on stage and in rehearsal with us felt really smothering. His style hadn't evolved much since the seventies, and he was convinced that the "young people today" were still looking for epic twelve-bar guitar solos.

I tried for weeks to find a way to provide a graceful exit for him from the band. I was carrying a significant amount of internal conflict about it. I finally worked up the courage to tell him that having him in the band was stressing me out.

In nearly five years of ministry together, I'd never once stood up to Ken. He was the mentor and I was his protégé. There was no room for role reversal or insubordination.

It happened during a board meeting that we'd held at my home. One of the board members asked for an update on the band, and I gave it. I updated where we'd been travelling and touched on a couple of personnel changes. Then I detailed the part about feeling smothered by Ken.

He appeared genuinely shocked and immediately offered to resign. I thanked him profusely. I felt like I'd misjudged him. Had I been wrong to bring it up in front of the board? He took it so well. I'd been carrying this tension for nearly the entire time he'd joined the band nearly six months earlier. I was so relieved that it was over.

Except it wasn't over. It took him nearly six months to actually let it go. He acted like everything was fine, but any time some kind of stress would arise from the musical side of the ministry, he'd remind me passive-aggressively that things would have gone much differently had he still be involved. He'd say things like this but follow up by informing me he was far too busy to play a part now.

It was like he was playing hard to get. Conversations like that made me not want to tell him when we were recording, which, in the end, only made matters worse.

Recording in studio was one of the most interesting experiences of my life to that point. My cousin owns his own studio, so we were blessed to be able to hang out with him for eighteen days while we created art. Throughout the process, we played and sang with everything we had, gathering each morning at six a.m. for breakfast where we'd pray, talk about God, and discuss the art we were making.

For the first couple days, we laid down scratch tracks for each of the original worship songs we'd crafted, a basic version of each song to give us a guide as to speed and feel.

We worked for two more weeks, family and friends dropping in to observe as bass, guitars, keyboards, and finally vocals were added. Veronica had given birth to our firstborn daughter only two months prior, so these were long days to her sleepless nights. As it turns out, the exhaustion she felt during those three weeks of recording was only a preview of our ministry life to come.

I'd push her past her limits time and time again as Ken and I pursued aggressive ministry goals. It was the place of a woman to serve her husband; Veronica knew this and realized she would be laying down her life to serve my vision and thus Ken's.

My priorities in life (and thus our priorities in life) at the time were ministry, work and family, in that order. I would drag Veronica and our baby girl around a lot that year under the guise of ministry. And when our second daughter was born only thirteen months later, nothing changed. I continued to be driven in the pursuit of ministry, and my family just had to keep up. If I could go back and be the husband and father I should have been to these precious women, I would. I guess the next best thing I can do is be there for them now.

I remember when the album was finally ready for release, and the time came for me to share our work with Ken. It wasn't hard to sense his displeasure that we didn't do it his way or include him in the process. He was quick to criticize the skill level of our guitar players and wasn't shy in letting me know that it wasn't "rocky" enough. It hurt, but I was used to taking a certain level of what he called constructive criticism. As a father, albeit a spiritual one, hurting my feelings only to lift my spirits again was one of his methods of control.

When I told him we were planning a CD release concert and that he was invited to open the night up with prayer, he seemed honored, but it was by opening that door I unknowingly relinquished control. As it happened, our big night was hijacked and became a spur-of-the-moment speaking engagement. He even requested an offering be taken in support of the ministry.

We played our songs, but our vision of a fun night sharing the music we'd created with family and friends had been replaced with his own agenda, complete with a message and alter call, much to our embarrassment and the confusion of our invited guests.

Eventually, Veronica and I learned that our art was really just an opening act to break the ice and create an atmosphere for something more important, the preaching of the word of God. We also learned that any time Ken "had a word" he could interrupt our most passionate experiences in the presence of God. Fortunately, years later we would unlearn it again and return to the expression of art as an act of worship in and of itself, the simple fulfillment of the gifts and talents God has created in us.

I had to ask myself, "Would I rather be told how to live my life to the fullest or watch and observe someone as they did just that?" I wanted the latter.

That smothering feeling I'd felt a couple years earlier while trying to lead my band with him on the stage? On the night we released our worship album it came back with a vengeance, and that is when it began threatening to suffocate me.

8

THE MISSION OF SUBMISSION

From time to time, Ken would contact us from wherever he and his family were ministering at the time. Generally speaking, his emails would express some type of correction, admonishment or, on rare occasions, a simple word of encouragement. Later on we realized there was always a reason behind these communications, a specific motivation or agenda, but at the time we were naive disciples.

In 2007, Ken and Diane invited us to visit them in Mexico—not as a missions trip but just to grow as friends. It had been nearly a year since we'd last spent any significant time with them. We agreed and packed up our things, including our musical instruments and some recording equipment. After feeling guilty for excluding Ken from our last recording project, I wanted to at least share the songs we'd been writing and working on since our album had been released.

We spent a week in Mexico, indoors. On our first missions trip, I discovered Ken wasn't really into playing or relaxing. During this visit, I realized nothing had changed. We could see the ocean from where we stayed, but we didn't visit it once. This nearly drove Veronica mad. We'd left our kids with my parents and were spending a week in Mexico, but we were not going to the beach. Fortunately, there was a pool, so Veronica would take Ken and Diane's kids to the pool and ignore the fact that I was spending the week inside.

It's hard to believe, but during the days, all we did was spend time fiddling with his wifi and working on other computer issues, all the while continuing a conversation centered around our displeasure with the state of our church back home.

The evenings, though, were pretty special. We had the undivided attention of the people we'd grown to admire. These people were living examples of what we had been taught was the ultimate sacrifice, a life dedicated to the service of the Lord.

Because we were still all members of the same church back home, we had a lot to talk and complain about. We didn't really consider these conversations gossip, since we were just pointing out problems and considering ways in which we could do church better.

We talked about the problems with the church today. We talked about the future. We talked about how we'd improve the church by following the example of the early church.

Ken had a lot of bitterness for the leaders there. He hated the politics and bureaucracy. He was basically ministering independent of our "home church" and running everything through our ministry.

For dinner one evening, we visited a popular local steakhouse. We had an incredible time, talking and dreaming of the future. Ken and I built grand plans to minister together until we were old men. Veronica and Diane just smiled and observed our passion.

After we left the restaurant, we wandered through an open-air night market. Veronica and I strolled hand in hand behind our friends, and as we walked, we found a small carving: a romantic figurine depicting a couple embracing, nude. It would be great for our bedroom, we thought, but Ken and Diane had become like mentors, and based on our understanding of their views on nudity and sexuality, we both could predict the disapproval of our hosts were they to find out.

I sent Veronica ahead to keep a look out and distract our friends should they turn around. I paid full price for the statuette, which probably caught the street vendor by surprise for a moment. The insistent, even panicked, way in which I shoved the cash towards the vendor, my hands and arms flailing as I tried to explain in English that I needed it wrapped quickly, probably didn't actually get us out of there any sooner.

Why did we feel such guilt over such a beautiful piece of art? Perhaps it was all the talk of modesty or maybe the dress codes from our previous missions trips together. Perhaps it was the way our friends believed in a higher moral standard and tried to teach us to do the same, to avoid any behavior that could potentially cause anyone to "stumble" by feeling justified upon observing that same or similar behavior in us.

In addition to the modesty issue, we knew that they were against drinking alcohol and also had a particular issue with swearing and movies that depicted any kind of romance or sexuality.

We quickly made our purchase, slipped it into the large purse Veronica had been carrying, and hurried to catch up, smiling and laughing, hoping to mask the guilt on our faces. I believe we were successful, but the dangerous seed of independent thought had begun to germinate, leaving us in conflict even though we didn't realize we were.

On the last night of our stay, we brought out the instruments and shared the intimate songs of worship we'd been working on over the last year, and we shared our desire to record again.

After enduring yet another conversation reminding me of the mistake I'd made in asking Ken to leave the band, and yet another reminder that he was too busy to join now so leaving the band was actually a good thing, we began to share our new songs with him and Diane.

Having my emotions lifted and dashed several times took a lot out of me. It was like riding an emotional roller coaster. One moment we'd feel like close friends and even peers, while the next we might feel as though we were children being punished for failing our parents' expectations.

One by one, we presented our art, open to the "honest, constructive criticism" we'd become accustomed to. I felt small and vulnerable as we sang and played the songs we were so passionate about only a week earlier. I felt as though I wasn't really any good as a musician or as a songwriter because Ken always had a better idea.

Looking up to him as a spiritual father didn't help matters. It felt as though he were superior to me in every way. My confidence had been shattered.

Though I'm sure there was some positive, encouraging feedback, and I don't remember being really scarred by the lack of encouragement, we never did work up the courage to record another album while submitted under his authority.

We'd spent all week fixing computers and bitching about the current state of the church and then capped it off with a critical evaluation of our ability to represent the ministry as worship leaders. It felt like we'd failed our evaluation.

After an emotionally exhausting week, Veronica and I actually changed our plans and left a day early, booking a night in a nice hotel to relax and unwind together. We'd been off work and away from our kids for over a week but had barely seen each other.

It was during this alone time that we began to examine how legalistic and judgmental Ken and Diane really were and how much more we would have to become if we were to fit in. In stepping back, we began to see the cult-like setting we had fallen into. We weren't free to think or have an opinion. We weren't allowed to go against the flow in virtually any way. We were beginning to wonder if it was oppressive. The best way I can describe the feeling we had as we left was the relief of breathing deeply after being trapped in a confined space filled with negativity and criticism.

Even though we both had fairly negative experiences, we still felt led to serve this couple. Even when we could see the control mechanisms, we couldn't step away from them. All roads were leading to a life where we'd continue to minister together for many years to come.

And yet, Veronica and I were changing. We could tell we were changing because we could see the things we used to believe still alive and well in our friends. We could tell we were changing because the things we were thinking and feeling were things we were afraid to share with our friends.

Where we would see beauty, they would cast judgment. Where we could see love, they only saw sin. Where we believed in equality, they believed in a clear, absolute truth; a dividing line between sinner and saved.

The question began to come to the forefront. Would we be able to learn and grow, expand our horizons, while remaining submitted to the couple we'd committed to serve? The call to serve overrode this concern.

~

Nearly a year later, after visiting them in Mexico, Ken invited me to join him in Lakeland, Florida for a series of "signs and wonders" revival meetings that had been going on for months and were growing in popularity. It was at this event that my passion for ministry exploded.

As I'd been feeling somewhat spiritually dry, I agreed to meet him and flew down the following week. I was hoping to reconnect, both with Ken and with God. One on one, our relationship was different than when we were with our spouses or our families. During our first meal together, Ken asked how my spiritual walk was going. Wanting to be honest and hoping for advice on how to grow, I admitted I was feeling pretty dry lately.

He then asked about the type of music I'd been listening to. He already knew from previous conversations of my growing disdain for contemporary Christian music, so I could tell he had an agenda with his line of questioning. As soon as I told him the type of music I'd been listening to, he made this clicking sound with his tongue, signaling his disapproval.

We argued nearly all day on the topic, ending with me finally acquiescing and agreeing to listen to more popular Christian music when I returned home to Canada.

Once I'd demonstrated the appropriate submission, we had a much better weekend. We decided to skip the first service and skip off to Disneyworld instead. Now, that sounded fun to me! Suddenly, once I'd shown honor to Ken, it was like we were best friends. Off to the Magic Kingdom we went, running around like kids. We had a blast. It was moments like this that caused me to overlook much of the glaring incongruence between the way I was seeking to live and the way Ken lived.

The next night, we went to the revival meetings. Ken spent most of the time mingling with other ministers, networking, and I did what any good disciple-slash-protégé would do. I carried his bag. When we finally did find our way to our reserved seats in the second row, I let the worship leader guide me into the presence of God.

As much as I've since been emotionally scarred by worship and the way music can be used to manipulate feelings, during this worship service all I can remember is singing and crying and being passionately inspired. I felt sincerely changed. I could sense the presence of God for the first time in a long time. It hit me hard, and I hit my knees.

For at least two songs I kneeled on the hard, cold concrete of the arena floor with my hands reached up to heaven. I didn't sing, I just felt. As the music played, I could feel God near me.

During the worship service, while I'd been kneeling with hands raised, Ken took my hand and prayed and twisted my wedding ring over and over. I didn't know what it meant to him at the time, but it creeped me out. As he twisted the ring that represented my sacred connection to Veronica, I first felt like he was somehow stealing from me. Every time he twisted my ring I felt violated. I shook off the ill feelings and focused on trusting him.

As the worship band continued to play, I remained on the floor of my row, kneeling in worship. Ken continued to stand over me, holding my outstretched hands and twisting my wedding ring. I thought of a story that is told during wedding ceremonies about how people used to believe there was a vein that ran straight to the heart from the ring finger.

I shuddered.

To this day, any time my ring twists on my finger, I get the same feeling.

Though things were starting to feel incredibly positive, there was still the underlying seed of conflict Veronica and I had identified the year before. There was this sense that something was "off."

Eventually Ken released my hands and went off to speak with one of the important talking heads visiting the revival meetings that day. I shook off the weird feelings from the ring experience and chose to trust that my mentor had only intended good to come of this particular action, and I also chose to believe the good I'd experienced on this particular trip far outweighed this small distraction.

Ken and I left the stadium, and I felt like I was walking on air. Ken warned me that God was taking me on a journey from which I'd never return, that I'd never be the same again. He encouraged me to bring the fullness of my experience in worship back to the people of our home church.

I felt inspired and empowered to carry out his mandate. I couldn't wait to bring true, passionate worship to our congregation again.

9

IN A BLAZE OF GLORY OR THE WORSHIP BOMB

Stepping off the plane upon my return home to Canada after receiving a life-changing shot of spiritual adrenaline, I felt like I was a disciple on a mission from God. I grew up in the church and had participated in many ultra-charismatic youth camps and retreats; I knew what a spiritual high felt like and how quickly it could fade. But this feeling was different. This time I wouldn't just be reacting to the experiences I'd had in Florida but recreating them here in my hometown. Revival was coming, and it was riding on me.

Overall, my time with Ken in Lakeland resulted in a rejuvenated vision for seeing people connected to God. The dryness I had been feeling and had talked about with him near the start of my trip was gone, my spirit refreshed. I carried a lot of anticipation about what would happen next. Ken encouraged me to let go of my inhibitions and "just go for it" as a worship leader. Reluctantly, I returned home, and he returned to whichever country he and Diane were based in at the time. I sensed something had changed, but I was nervous to carry that change back to my church in Canada.

As teenagers riding the bus home after a three day church youth retreat in euphoric jubilation, we would usually respond to the "never be the same again" feeling by making a series of promises to God and each other because we'd encountered the presence of God in such a concentrated way. "I'll do my devotions every day," "I'll pray every hour," and "I'll only watch movies recommended by my pastor" were the kind of commitments we'd make before God and our accountability partners.

Though I knew I would never be the same again, I didn't know how that would look. Veronica noticed the change in me right away, but like me, she couldn't put her finger on it either.

Travelling between Lakeland, Florida and my hometown near Vancouver, BC, Canada was a great reminder of the growing distance between two ministry "worlds" I was living between at the time. On one hand was my allegiance to Ken and the new parachurch ministry we were creating; on the other was the local church and leadership of whom Veronica and I were still "under the covering." Ken encouraged me to go home and "give it all I got," but part of me knew I'd be breaking boundaries. And with Ken and Diane not there for support, I would be pushing the envelope on my own.

Veronica and I were primarily ministering weekly as volunteer worship pastors at our home church, but our worship album was released under the parachurch ministry I was leading with Ken. There was definitely some confusion and tension as to where our allegiance lay. The pastor of our church at the time had some concerns and used a verse from the book of Matthew, chapter 6 verse 24 to make his point: "No one can serve two masters. Either you will hate the one and love the other, or you will be devoted to the one and despise the other."

I felt like a child of divorce, pulled between the explosive energy of a man with whom I'd just spent a week in Florida and the consistent, predictable leadership of the church I'd been born into. It didn't really matter to me which ministry "owned" us as long as we continued to experience amazing opportunities, travelling and leading worship in churches all over the west coast while also ministering regularly in our local church back home whenever we could.

I arrived home from Lakeland on a Thursday night, spiritually energized and ready to ignite the passionate worship bomb I carried with me on the plane. I could barely contain my excitement as I anxiously awaited our next opportunity to lead worship and/or change the world. Little did I know, the bomb would explode in both a powerful and destructive way.

Sunday rolled around, and as was our routine most weeks, at 6a.m. I packed up the band trailer and headed to the church. I usually spent the first couple hours setting up, praying, and picking songs, and this week was no different. Although, somehow I knew that the service was going to be different than we were used to.

The rest of the band showed up at 8a.m. and we ran through our pre-service rehearsal, checking sound levels, and shuffling the song list around. By 9:15, we wrapped up the practice, I slipped out to pick up Veronica and the girls, and we all met backstage at about 9:45.

Once we finished getting the girls set up in Sunday school, we met the rest of our team backstage behind the curtain. As was our preservice custom, most of us now chased back the coffee we'd consumed during rehearsal with an energy drink. For years we'd found the Holy Spirit at the bottom of a Red Bull can. Leading worship for an experienced congregation in a charismatic environment can really take it out of you. It takes a lot of energy to play a rock show at 10a.m. on a Sunday morning.

Our sound tech popped back to bring us each a bottle of water and to join us in prayer before we went out there. Each week, the worship leader would attempt to inspire the team before we began, and this week was no different. Veronica remembers the pep talk I gave that morning better than I do, but I do remember encouraging our team to touch heaven, to bring heaven down and worship God like nothing had happened before the service and like nothing was planned after the service.

At ten in the morning on Sunday, May 4th, 2008, we began a worship service I would never forget. We felt God moving in us, as musicians, like never before. We started the service like usual. Veronica wanted me to speak about what I believed God had been doing in me since Florida, but I resisted. I could sing, play and prophesy from behind the safety of my piano, yet I was extremely uncomfortable speaking. Veronica would nearly always give the opening exhortation to psych the worshippers up and get them on their feet.

I used to lead worship with my eyes closed nearly the entire service. My hands would fly over the keyboard, but I'd rarely peek. It was my way of hearing the words and music we were playing and connecting directly to the heart of God. On this particular morning, after we played our first song, I felt like there was a spiritual wall in the room. It felt like a thick pane of glass that was keeping us as a congregation from experiencing God the way I had only days before in Florida.

I'd experienced things like this before in ministry. Years earlier, as a fairly novice worship leader, I perceived a similar "blockage" during worship at a youth event and discerned that we weren't experiencing the fullness of the presence of God because we weren't desperate enough, we weren't "pressing in" hard enough. On one occasion, I called out the entire second row of youth in attendance at a worship gathering and loudly exhorted them to "respect God and stop fooling around!" Even though I wasn't the most confident public speaker, I had felt like there had been a holy, righteous anger welling up within me.

I felt the same way while leading worship the Sunday after Lakeland as I had felt years earlier as leader of the youth band. These people just weren't desperate for God. If they only knew that they could experience the presence of God like I had only days before, they wouldn't be standing in front of me just going through the motions! I wasn't going to call out our congregation out like I had done years before in youth group, but the perceived wall was making me angry. What was it? Apathy? Boredom? Sin? Were we wasting our time?

I paused our worship set and prayed. I prayed over the congregation that the walls would be broken, that our words would be heard in heaven and that heaven be heard and felt on earth, in this room. Then we resumed the worship service.

BOOM.

The passionate worship bomb I'd brought home from my experiences in Lakeland detonated, exploding with a blaze of glory. The walls were broken and the floodgates opened. It was unlike anything that had ever happened in this community, but it was a lot like Lakeland. It was alive. We played through our set of worship songs like we'd never play again. We'd broken through. The tangible presence of God had filled the room, and it was awesome.

I sustained a chord on my piano with my right hand but otherwise stood motionless. At the end of the most intense set we'd ever played, we continued to wait on God while not one person moved. For several minutes we waited. It felt like the air in that high school gymnasium-turned-church-sanctuary was heavy, thick with tense anticipation. As a congregation, we were waiting to see if we'd take another step deeper into this electric experience in the presence of God.

Slowly, I began to feel a cadence, like a heartbeat, deep within my body. As we stayed nearly motionless, my hands began to play again, this rhythm now being expressed through the keys on my piano. It was an enveloping, throbbing, pulsing musical expression. Our drummer seemed to feel it too and started matching my passion, praying and crying at the same time. Other members of the band began to hear and feel the music, and for twenty minutes we just played, basking in the ecstatic presence of God.

I'd never felt as reverent or as awestruck by God as I did that morning. The associate pastor nearly exploded from his seat and began to dance. He didn't do a typical, conservative, twist-your-waist-but-don't-move-your-feet pastor dance either. He danced like a maniac in worship before the Lord.

Others started sharing words and songs, our music undergirding it all, the rhythm building in intensity. Someone gave a word that encouraged the congregation to be more like children, then two other pastors got up and shared incredible, inspiring words. Veronica suddenly started running around the auditorium, like really running, praying while circling the people and really stirring things up. People were dancing in the aisles, kneeling in their seats or laying full out on the floor. The experience I had in the presence of God in Florida had nothing on this.

What happened in Florida was a personal experience; it was for me alone. But this was for our local church. This was for my family. I was witnessing and participating as nearly four hundred adults encountered God in communion with one another. I felt like I had been personally called by God to bring his people closer to him.

As a fairly charismatic church, we were used to vibrant worship services. Our worship times were usually fairly loud and consisted of a lot of moving parts. Hand clapping, hand raising, dancing, shouting, jumping, crying, and laying flat out on the floor were not unusual expressions.

However, a worship service so engaging that the order of service was overridden and the announcements were foregone and the sermon was cut short was unusual. In fact, I only know of two other times in the twenty-five years I'd attended this particular church in which worship took up the entire two-hour time slot. It looked like we were headed straight for the finish line as there were only fifteen minutes remaining in the service scheduled to conclude at noon. The bomb fragments were now ready to wreak havoc.

I remember opening my mouth to lead us in another song of praise when the band kind of crashed out of sync and faded out. Shocked, I opened my eyes and looked back at our bass player and drummer to see what was going on. Both of them sort of sheepishly gestured to the senior pastor who was in charge of the service that day. Standing silhouetted in the stage lights, the pastor stood, his fist clenched tightly in the nearly universal hand signal for ending a worship song. We had been summoned to stop, and it was dramatic.

It felt like the pastor's closed fist had just punched me in the stomach, leaving me gasping for air. Veronica looked like she'd awoken from a dream and was caught standing naked in front of five hundred people.

Years later, she would explain that is exactly what it felt like for her.

"Worship can be like an out of body experience for me. It's like feeling, touching, smelling, tasting. It's an exquisite sensation that can only be likened to sex, a lost-in-the-moment kind of intensity," she said.

When she worships, it's less about lyric, melody and rhythm and more about aligning her body with the spirit of God—feeling, touching and communing with the nearly tangible presence of God.

The tangible feeling of the divine had that day been sucked from the room, leaving her, and the rest of us, exposed. The bright stage lights illuminated our terror.

We'd worshipped for nearly an hour and forty-five minutes. The service was scheduled to end in just over ten more. Why would anyone take control, rein in what was happening between the people and spirit of God, so they could rush through a sermon entitled "Jesus Is More Important Than Angels"? The pastor we'd grown up with our entire lives rushed through his message, touching on fewer than half of his nine points in the ten minutes we had left, getting everyone out the building in time for lunch.

As we sat down in the front row, somewhat dazed after spending such a long time in the presence of God, I could barely hear the fragment of a sermon our senior pastor was delivering. I felt angry and embarrassed that our senior pastor had interfered with what God was clearly doing in the people of our congregation through us, his servants. It felt like he had stolen away my destiny, my God-ordained purpose. My heart was screaming, "Why, God? Why?!" We were left feeling like the rug had pulled out from under us. We'd laid it all out there, everything we had, believing that God had been trying to reach out and touch his people, calling us to break the tradition and turn our hearts towards him.

We'd never experienced such a passionate expression of worship in the church we called home in our entire lives. I could barely stand up while we played through the last half of the service. In that moment, I knew things could never be the same for the church we were serving as worship leaders. Initially, it appeared that the preset agenda and the maintenance of the status quo were more important. When the man with a plan stole the moment away, our hopes that had soared with the spirit only moments before now crashed with a clatter to the floor. I had believed God was going to use me to ignite a new passion in the collective hearts of our congregation. This belief was shattered and hope lost when even after the most intimate worship experience of our lives, it was still business as usual.

Veronica and I returned home after the service, put the kids down for their afternoon naps, and laid on the couches in our living room. We were stunned. For nearly two hours we lay awake, speechless, while our children slept peacefully in their rooms. When they awoke, we walked them down the stairs, prepared their snacks and let them watch movies until bedtime.

I felt hurt, vulnerable and stripped of dignity. Veronica vowed to never let herself get lost in the presence of God like that again in order to avoid such devastating embarrassment. She was angry that God didn't protect us. We both felt like we'd given it everything, we'd broken through the barriers keeping us as a church from experiencing the fullness of God's presence.

We tried for days to understand what happened. We couldn't fathom how this could have happened, how the walls of the man-made box of religion containing the presence of God had been shattered only to be rebuilt in time to end the church service.

We were emotionally exhausted, our hearts crushed. In the days that followed, we were informed by an email from church leadership that they had been inundated with complaints about the way the service had gone.

The email from one of my favorite pastors at the time continued with this winning line: "When the Holy Spirit moves, all hell breaks loose." Yes, it appeared so. Our pastor proceeded to inform us the events of that particular Sunday morning were a rare, one-time event, and we couldn't expect God to move in that type of way on an ongoing basis.

I rejected the notion that God couldn't move passionately and prophetically on a continual basis. I had seen it in Lakeland. It was breaking out in the here and now, in our community. But I knew the pastor didn't want to lose his precious pulpit time. It was his purpose and meaning for the church. So instead of continuing a theological debate, we simply bowed our heads and walked away.

I felt compelled to call Ken, a conversation that would later become incredibly ironic. He advised me only days earlier to come home to this church and give it all I had. I wished he had been able to see how I'd heeded the advice he had given me in Lakeland and worshipped God with wild abandon. I was able to connect with him the next day while he was in an airport between speaking engagements. We spoke for nearly an hour about the tragic, closed-minded and reactionary response by the church leadership. I asked if he thought we should leave the church. It was clear to me that they obviously weren't really open to the move of God.

Ken helped me realize I was meant for more than this. We both agreed church was never supposed to be about man's agenda but about experiencing communion with God. After my conversation with Ken, I told Veronica we would be leaving our church for good. I'd decided it was time for us to leave the church we'd been born and raised in, the church both of our families still attended.

We'd gone out in a blaze of glory, giving it everything we had, holding nothing back.

Even if we wanted to, there was no way we could go back to the way things were. There was clearly something more, something greater, something more real. We'd tasted it. How could we settle for less?

We'd tasted and seen the goodness and the wonder of the presence of God. We couldn't simply choose to not pursue God in the same way. Given the choice to return to a meager, measured, glory-like substitute was like asking an adult to return to consuming canned baby food.

Given the choice, I decided Veronica and I would rather set out on our own to discover a place open to what God had in store.

10

CALLED FROM THE WILDERNESS

Nearly eight months passed since we had led the worship service that resulted in our departure from our home church. Leaving the church had proven to be emotionally challenging. Months later, we still felt isolated and alone.

It was New Year's Day, 2009. We'd slept in and were quietly padding down the carpeted stairs and onto the hardwood into the kitchen, being careful to tread lightly so as not to wake the girls.

Veronica began making coffee while I made the toast. As I reached for a couple of slices of multigrain, the flashing red light on our phone caught my attention. With the aroma of Starbucks dark roast wafting through the air, I pressed the button to retrieve a voicemail that must have been left for us while we slept.

"Wake up! O sleeper." Ken's voice jolted us from our state of relaxation. "Rise from the dead, and Christ will shine on you. Happy New Year! Love you guys."

Upon hearing his voice on the answering machine, I remember instantly feeling guilty yet inspired at the same time. To feel what we felt by receiving a message like that, you have to understand that we grew up in an environment where people took prophetic words very seriously without really checking them out or even checking in with ourselves.

Were we sleeping? Were we dead? Ken's words washed over us, renewing our desire for ministry. Of course we wanted Christ to shine on us. I felt inspired to change, to grow. Veronica felt it too.

To our surprise, Ken and Diane were about to move back to Canada permanently. I returned Ken's call later in the day, and he shared with me that they would need to find a car to rent or a cheap car to purchase upon moving home.

I knew what I needed to do.

Without consulting Veronica, I decided to give our late-model Chrysler 300 to the missionary family we loved so much. It would mean we'd have to purchase a new vehicle for ourselves, but I knew how much honor it would show Ken.

It was snowing when we pulled up the drive at Diane's parents' farm. Her parents were away. We parked the car and hid the key. We still hadn't told Ken and Diane, but I left a note describing the gift.

Veronica was not exactly on board with the idea of giving away our $10,000 car and purchasing a new one. Financially, it was a foolish decision.

Ken and Diane were floored, to say the least. We received such praise for our generosity. The gift reignited the depth and meaning of our relationship.

The next time I spoke with Ken, our discussion was centered on the need to create a "gathering" of believers who were ready and willing to do things differently. Together, we formed a vision to co-lead a church, Ken and Diane with Veronica and me. We planned to launch some type of weekly or biweekly meeting in the spring.

Our vision was deep and pure and true to the ways of Jesus as we understood them. Veronica and I proposed we include a meal and open conversation at each of our weekly meetings. It would be about building real relationships; it would be about creating family, something tangible that you could see, hear, taste, smell, and touch. We'd worship. We'd speak of God together. Ken wouldn't always be the one preaching. We'd "pass the mic" and have true "every member ministry."

While we knew we'd have to collect some money to cover expenses such as building rental, it was our intent to give away up to ninety percent of the money raised, using only ten percent inside the church. We planned on keeping our expenses small. In other words, no one would draw a salary. We'd all volunteer.

At the time, we really weren't sure if we'd even call it "church." There was so much baggage attached to that word. It was actually my idea to add church to the end of our ministry's name. I had faith that we were redeeming the concept of church, and as such, we'd be redeeming the word; plus, using the word "church" added legitimacy to our gatherings.

The vision was deeply inspired by what we had both experienced at Lakeland and in ministry. We wanted God to be at the forefront and community to be real. In hindsight, the vision was impractical but not impossible. I would have given everything I had for a community like that to exist.

Several months later, we were given an opportunity to rent the basement from the Lutheran church one evening a week for about a hundred and fifty dollars. We had a couple of signs printed and mounted to some old wooden sawhorses and placed them out by the road.

About seventy people had responded to our invitation to join us for our "gathering" on that first Friday night.

Our intention was to create a true community of followers of Jesus. Worship would not be something to watch; there would be no aspect of performance. In the beginning, Veronica and I led our times of worship with just our voices and my piano. We enjoyed such simple times in the presence of God.

We opened our inaugural service by covering a popular Justin Timberlake song at the time about "finding our way back home" and about the "old me" being "dead and gone." Our worship on that first night was pretty raw and very real.

After the way we'd left our previous church, with an emotionally explosive musical bang, we felt like it was time to keep things simple for a while. I remember Veronica speaking out before our time of worship by talking about the long, tough journey we'd been on.

Every thing Veronica and I did and felt in that brightly-lit church basement on that first Friday night was pure and felt holy. Our intentions were untainted by the production church had once been to us. There was no sign of the box we'd been taught to store the Holy Spirit in while not in use.

One of the other songs we sang that night was Rita Springer's "It's Gonna Be Worth It." The hard, painful journey we'd been on—the dry, desert season that we were only just emerging from— we knew it was all going to be worth it. We'd found an oasis that would become our church, our family and our friends. Our faith was stirred up; there was limitless potential in this place. We'd finally found home.

Those nights were so sweet. We were experiencing "church" for the first time in a way we could actually reconcile with our understanding of the ways of Jesus.

Since leaving our first church and throughout our time in "the wilderness," outside of any church in particular, I had begun a blog about our spiritual journey. It was my intention to share from the heart about the questions we were asking, the battles we were facing and our search for a better church. About a month before we held our first gathering, I'd written a blog post about the problems with church and my excitement about the future:

> We've learned to lean on the church (the institution) as a crutch, or maybe as a pill; a way for us to get all of our spiritual needs and obligations met and fulfilled in one place, in one or two hours. Get in, get 'er done, get out. This is where I want to shift my mindset. Stop doing church, stop (merely) going to church, and start being the church. This is what we were called to be!
>
> I wish you could hear my laughter as I write; excited, mischievous, nervous all at once. Ha ha! We are getting closer! Love God, and love people. Do it on your own time too, not just in a once-a-week, pre-allotted two hour time period. Amen.

I was so excited about the way things were going to be. I knew we were finally going to experience church the way it was meant to be experienced. We felt like our journey to find church was over and we'd arrived at last.

In reality, our journey was only just beginning.

11

THE COVENANT

In the months leading up to the launch of our weekly gatherings, I did something I would come to deeply regret in the years that followed, something that would later cause me great pain and confusion.

Ken had become like a hero to me, speaking into my life, causing to me to believe in myself and in a vision of the future where we could change the world together through our ministry.

The organization we'd founded together was primarily a missions organization, and I was flattered to be chosen to be part of it. I jumped in at the ground floor and quickly rose to the second highest position in the hierarchy, given the flashy titles of Senior Associate Leader and Secretary-Treasurer.

During the foundational years, some time after we led two missions trips to Mexico but before we visited him and Diane in Mexico as friends, Ken invited me to join him for coffee on a Tuesday night. I always felt so honored to be invited to spend some one-on-one time with the man I called a spiritual father.

It was on this coffee date that he proposed a more formal mentorship-type relationship, an opportunity for me to open up and ask for help or advice. He was offering to be there for me, and I accepted his offer. We started meeting every other Tuesday night, just to talk about God, marriage, ministry and life. I felt that it was a great thing, getting insight and advice from a man whom I looked up to.

Veronica thought it was a wonderful idea, even though she often felt inferior or second to Ken. Being mentored in this way would help me become a better man to lead our home. She was as honored as I was with the idea.

As the years went on, Ken would come and go from various short- and long-term missions engagements, but our meetings would continue on a fairly regular basis. We'd usually meet at a local Starbucks around eight in the evening, staying until they closed and kicked us out.

We spent a lot of time talking about pursuing God and living a life on the "highway of holiness." Basically, we talked about the things we should and shouldn't do as Christians. He taught me to live as an example and how I must learn to be careful to live in such a way so as not to cause others to stumble. He became a veritable life-coach, accountability partner and mentor.

These regularly scheduled meetings went on for at least a couple of years. We grew as friends, dreaming and developing vision for the future.

A funny thing happened after a while (funny in a concerning, unsettling sense). Veronica noticed I was coming home more frustrated than when I'd left for these meetings. I was irritable, controlling and driven.

I had also become extremely defensive about my mentor. When Veronica reflected back to me the way I would behave after returning home from our weekly meetings, I would snap at her, explaining in a less than gentle way that she didn't know what she was talking about.

If I had been honest with her, or even with myself, I would have been forced to admit I was suppressing some frustration with Ken. The focus of our mentorship meetings had changed. In the beginning, there was a lot more mentorship and a lot less ministry talk. Eventually, our times together basically turned into ministry management meetings mixed with a little personal manipulation.

I was no longer getting the one-on-one support from Ken I'd grown accustomed to. I was now in the supporting role, trying to serve the man in any way I could.

I never let Veronica see the struggle I was having with Ken. She expected I was getting together with Ken every other week to be mentored and to grow. If I had told her we were merely handling the affairs of the ministry, she would have just as soon preferred me to stay home with her.

As leaders of a growing ministry, there were always big issues to be dealt with. Some of the crises involved members of our band, whom Veronica and I were still ministering with at the time. On one occasion, we received a report from a concerned Christian friend that a band member, covered by our ministry, had been seen drinking alcohol in a local restaurant, something that was seen as taboo. In addition, we discovered he'd become quite involved in swing dancing, and upon further investigation, we learned that alcohol was served at his dancing events as well.

Ken gave me the responsibility to bring corrective action to this band member, to discipline my friend. Exhibiting swift and sure leadership, I fired my friend from the band for the sin that was in his life. The soft sorrow in his eyes as I delivered my well-practiced words of justice nearly swayed me, but I was convinced it was for the best. Maybe some time outside of our fellowship would bring about change in my friend's life.

I didn't catch it for a long time. In that moment, I thought I was doing a good thing. I was being a good Christian, a good disciple, learning to be a leader by submitting to a leader who was willing to pour into me. Ken made it clear throughout the mentoring process that I was special, that he would never spend this much time and energy with just anyone.

It was all about honor.

In later years, circumstances and theological beliefs would change and allow my weekly meetings with Ken to take place in licensed establishments, and instead of discussing the ins and outs of ministry over non-fat lattes, we did so over double-tall rum & cokes.

Only recently did I work up the courage to invite my old friend and band-mate, now married, to join Veronica and me for dinner at a local steakhouse. When the waitress came to take our drink order, I ordered my usual rum & Coke while Veronica ordered a glass of merlot. They also ordered drinks from the bar, and I'm not sure if they caught the ironic subtlety of the moment, but I did.

During the meal, I worked up the courage to repent of my actions years earlier. I'd carried much guilt over the years because of the things I had done on behalf of the ministry. The tears in my eyes were mirrored in the eyes of my old friend, and God's love flowed freely, covering over and washing away my presumptive, judgmental, sinful deed. Redemption is beautiful like that. While we can't change the past, redemption changes our own judgment of the events of the past and thus affects our future.

I've since been able to assemble the moments of manipulation that all fell under the guise of "mentorship." I remember the first time it happened—the first time he crafted a conversation to achieve a specific result. I would observe his powers of mental manipulation over the next few years.

The scars of the first time I was spiritually abused and mentally manipulated are still visible today.

I didn't recognize the manipulative control at first. The initial moments were subtle. One week, Ken would talk about how there were some very successful ministries being built on two or three leaders who were dedicating themselves to one another, making covenants to never separate. Because of this commitment, they were unstoppable.

In a subsequent meeting, he would take it a step further, suggesting it was the junior or associate leader who needed to make a lifelong "covenant" to support the vision of the senior for there really to be success. He told me he was looking for young men to rise up and surround him. He envisioned an entourage that would travel with him when he went and ministered in other cities, a group of sons he would father and pour into.

My heart leaped. This was my moment. I had a chance to be his first-born spiritual son. Still, it was never a proposition; he would never ask me to make a covenant to him. It was all about the younger approaching the older and making such a covenant.

He'd made it abundantly clear as he set up the rules for covenant by telling me stories of ministers we both knew who had benefitted from the covenant-type relationship. It was time for me to get some skin in the game. My spirit jumped at the chance.

I don't think I planned for it to happen in advance. Maybe it was just time. Maybe it was inevitable. Maybe it was Ken's plan all along. Maybe I'd been groomed for "such as time as this."

It was about quarter after eight, and I was running late for our regularly scheduled meeting. We had just recently begun to plan for the launch of the weekly church "gatherings" as we were calling them at the time, and we had ramped up the frequency of our meetings. Instead of every other Tuesday night, we were now meeting weekly at 8p.m. on Mondays. I pulled into the parking lot in my big white Dodge Ram pickup and backed into the spot next to where his brand new Ford F-350 was already parked. It took me two tries to get my truck backed in, perfectly centered between a dirty white panel van and his navy blue pick-up.

I wanted so badly to impress him in anything and everything I did. To my chagrin, I looked up to see him seated at a table by the window at our usual Starbucks and realized he had been watching me park.

"Couldn't quite get it in one shot, huh?" he joked as I walked through the door.

I laughed it off and hugged him, and we made our way to place our drink orders with the barista. I was still kicking myself, embarrassed I had failed to impress him with my parking prowess. I remember thinking; I'll have to work on that.

I ordered my usual Quad Venti, Extra Hot, Non-fat Hazelnut Latte. He perused the menu board for several moments, asking about which drinks "had coffee in them" before settling on a vanilla latte. Though we did this every week, the routine was basically the same.

We sat back down together at our usual round wooden table by the window. For a while, Ken talked about the vision we were about to implement in the following weeks, a gathering of the saints like we'd never seen before: A kingdom-principled church.

"Of course, it will only be possible if a core of dedicated people rise up, and those leaders are led by an inner core of trusted leaders who will be positioned most closely to me," Ken said, explaining the leadership structure of our new church.

I was completely blind to the practically blasphemous, cultish hierarchy we were setting up. All I could see at the time was that I needed to be in that "inner-core." I needed to be at the top of it all, standing at the right hand of Pastor Ken.

I felt like everything was becoming clear. The prophetic word Ken had spoken over Veronica and me at our wedding, the intimate walk-on-water talk in Mexico, the years of mentorship, and the way he had helped guide us away from a church that he felt wasn't ready to receive the move of God: all of it was leading up to this moment.

I knew what I had to do.

Interrupting him as he spoke of the latest ministry issues, I grasped his hands, looked deeply into his eyes and pledged my allegiance to this man of God.

"Ken, I need you to know, here and now that I am here to see you flourish," I said, my voice carrying a tone of commitment and emotional sincerity. "Where you lead, I will follow. I will never leave you."

Never. I'd be the young, passionate protégé to this wise, experienced apostle. To really seal the deal and demonstrate my understanding of the covenant I was making, I drew comparison to covenants that had been made between other high profile ministers in famous churches and ministries of which we were both aware.

That evening in May, at a table by the window in our local Starbucks, I dedicated my life in a covenant to serve this man and his vision for the rest of my life.

We continued to grasp hands in silence. It was the first time I'd ever seen him speechless. His lower lip quivered a bit, and an intimate love surrounded us. He tried to speak, but his voice cracked due to the emotion of the moment.

After taking a sip of his latte, he continued.

"This changes everything," he said, his gaze filling me with potential. The tears flowed; we stood and embraced.

It would be nearly three years before I realized the true ramifications of my actions. Until that time, however, I would be celebrated, exalted, lifted up and used as a sermon illustration time after time. Looking back, I have to wonder why this covenant was so important to him. Knowing now what I didn't know then, I think he was pleased to have found someone who bought into his vision, that he'd groomed someone he could control. Did he do it intentionally? I don't know, but in the end, I think it came down to the fact that he needed something or someone to validate him and his ministry to provide credibility.

I returned home late that evening, and Veronica was already asleep in bed. It was several hours later than the time I told her I would be home. I tiptoed around the room and crawled into bed with care so as not to wake her. I was grateful to keep the covenant to myself, if only for the night.

When the beautiful woman awoke from her slumber, turned to me and asked how my night was, I told her it was good and kissed her forehead. Then she saw the clock and that it was well past midnight.

"Where have you been?" she asked, annoyed, "Why do you stay out so late with him?"

I told her of the covenant.

"What do you mean, you've dedicated yourself to serve him for the rest of your life? What does that even mean?" I gave her a few examples from the Bible and from ministries that we were both familiar with. She wasn't impressed; I'd have to work to teach her.

"This is weird," she said with a scowl. I couldn't tell if it was because I woke her up so late or if she didn't like the idea of the covenant. I didn't have to wonder long.

"So you're committed to both of us for life? I, as your wife, and he as—what? Your mistress?" She let the words hang there, before turning her back to me in dramatic fashion, attempting to fall back to sleep and forget about the covenant I'd made without even speaking to her of it beforehand.

"This is so weird, Travis," she mumbled, the last words she spoke to me that night.

I hadn't yet realized what this covenant actually meant. Something dark deposited in my soul that night wouldn't be chased away by the light of God's love for years. I might as well have surrendered the right to make decisions for myself. Little did I know, the decision I made that evening would come back to haunt me.

12

CELEBRATING COVENANT

After revealing the covenant to Veronica that night, we didn't speak of it much. It simply was. In reality, not much had changed, as we both knew I'd long since dedicated myself in both the Lord's and Ken's service. As she had done so many times before, Veronica resigned herself to the fact that if she wanted to honor me and honor God, she'd have to submit to both her husband and his mentor.

Suppressing her own passion was something she'd become well accustomed to doing. She hated the way Ken was able to so easily control me, the man she'd once known as an independent force, a rebel and a rule-breaker, but she saw it as the only way to maintain peace in our own covenant-bound relationship.

The covenant would become a convenient but oppressive mechanism for controlling me, but it worked because it also fed something within me. It fed my desire for honor. It fed my need for something real and permanent. But it also crippled me from speaking up, and this was the defining mechanism that allowed the oppression to continue.

Just after I made the covenant, Ken continually recognized me, week after week in our church services, as his right-hand man. I loved it when he honored me by telling the congregation of my dedication and of the covenant I'd made to serve his vision and the vision of "this house."

As our newly planted church began to grow, Ken spoke of a grand future when he would travel as an itinerant minister, being sent out from this house. I would nod in agreement, publicly demonstrating my support as he spoke of his vision to have a group of eight or ten young men who would travel with him.

I knew Ken was looking to pour into other spiritual sons, and while it made me jealous, I learned to accept it. He would often reassure me that even though there would be many more disciples like me, I would always be special. I'd be like his first-born spiritual son.

During our first few weekly services, Ken informed me that he would be needing a "body-man." This was someone who would help deflect people away before and after the services who were trying to get to him. Before services, he needed to spend time alone preparing, and he always felt drained after preaching. He didn't have the energy to give to the people who would often approach and want to talk after the service.

I'd seen leaders at some of the conferences we attended who had personal security, but Pastor Ken's request was a little strange to me. Our church only had fifty or so people in it at the time. Nonetheless, as his covenant-sworn protégé, I went to work recruiting more young men to rise up and serve Pastor Ken.

Some of the young leaders I approached felt uncomfortable with the directive Ken had tasked me with. One even went as far as to imply Ken was experiencing delusions of grandeur and ended up leaving the church over what he called an "absurd leadership culture." Undeterred, I pressed on, eventually enlisting four young men into what we called "The Guard of Honor."

I was starting to understand why Pastor Ken had given me this task with the strict instructions of making sure the people I approached believed the idea of personal protection for him was mine. He had said there would be more interest if the focus were about honor and not pride.

My strategy was more or less the same each time: "I'm feeling an urgency to protect Pastor Ken and, in turn, protect and build the church," I'd begin, engaging the attention of my new recruit. "He's said it many times, but I think we are getting to the breaking point. We've all gotta step up and carry the load, kinda like when Aaron and Hur held up Moses' arms during the battle against the Amalekites. You know what I mean?"

Without leaving too much room for questioning, I'd continue, "We must rise up as brothers and sons supporting a father. We need to delegate away some of the things that are sucking him away from his much-desired time with God. I think on this you'll agree, the more time he gets, the better he leads."

Once I had secured their commitments, I would detail the responsibility of a member of Ken's "Guard."

"Pre-service, Pastor Ken needs to disappear at least forty-five minutes before the service is set to begin, and he is to be escorted to a quiet room to prepare. He is to be escorted back out of his room and into the sanctuary just prior to the service. Even if he's mingling, one of us needs to be standing within five feet at all times. This is to protect his mind from being distracted by whatever random needs or thoughts get thrown at him pre-service."

I'd be certain to prepare my charges with the weightiness of the commitment, being sure they knew of the prophetic act they were carrying out by protecting the man of God who led us.

I was his personal assistant, confidant, protégé and friend. When he requested something of me, I did it. This was the culture of honor he preached of, this was the covenant we created. I didn't even think twice.

Even now, as I read through the demands I was tasked to relay to my "honor guard" troops, I am blown away that I couldn't see anything wrong with the culture of control we were immersed in. I had become just like Ken, controlling other men with a commitment of honor.

At the time, however, I was in my element. I served his vision with blind allegiance, and in turn many of my wishes for the church were granted. My dreams for a true, honest gathering of the followers of Jesus were coming true.

About six months after beginning our weekly gatherings, Veronica and I were invited to travel back to Lakeland, Florida, to the place where, two years earlier, so much had changed for me. Ken would be speaking at four separate events between December 30, 2009, and January 2, 2010, and he wanted us to come and lead worship at each of the services.

I was thrilled. This seemed like one of those "next level" or "shift" moments. In the charismatic, prophetic renewal movements, there is a lot of talk of "seasons and shifts." We'd often hear Ken speak in these terms.

"I sense that the next three months are going to be important. There is going to be a shift..." he'd begin, continuing with something like, "There is going to be a season of (hope, passion, dedication, intercession, giving, or whatever was popular at that moment), but it will only come to pass if we increase in (faith, prayer, tithing, unity...)."

Sometimes he'd prophesy multiple shifts. I remember an email I drafted with him for our weekly newsletter that we worded something like this:

"You can see the good 'shifts' or changes in others around you, but you cannot expect to 'shift' like them until you first seek Jesus and His desire for change in your own life. Then you will begin the 'shift' that He has for you, thus linking with the 'shifts' around you."

Looking back, I have no idea what this was even supposed to mean. At the time, I was buying what he was selling. All I knew was if there was going to be a "shift" while Ken was ministering in Florida, then I had to be there for it.

While we stood on the stage, singing original songs we'd written in front of an audience nearly four times the size of ours back home, I was on top of the world. We were living the dream. We'd arrived.

Veronica, however, was starting to wonder why we were doing all of this. Sure, it was fun to travel and minister with our friends, but on the other hand it just felt like another thing she was being dragged around to.

Our CD was available at the back on our ministry's "product" table, and we were treated like minor celebrities. When we walked into that venue on the first night, I knew the vision of travelling in ministry with an "entourage" was being fulfilled for Pastor Ken. Plus, for this new audience, I was a living, breathing example of the culture of covenant honor that he spoke of. That alone gave me bonus points with the local church leaders.

Each night we'd be taken out for a meal with some of the more prominent church leaders, and once again, my covenant to Pastor Ken was paraded about. We were a perfect example of unity and honor.

We flew home full of faith and a good measure of pride. We were even upgraded to first class, which we'd been conditioned to identify as a sign of God's favor.

Seventeen days after the thrill of ministering as quasi-celebrity guest ministers in Florida, I experienced my first instance of spiritual discipline under the terms of our covenant. Though I handled it with honor and grace, it would hardly be the last time control would creep into the covenant I'd committed to with Pastor Ken.

~

Just over a year earlier, around the time that Ken had left the "Wake Up O Sleeper" voicemail, I'd begun writing about faith. Sporadically throughout the year I posted on my blog about the things I was pondering. I was about to discover I needed to start running these personal writings past Pastor Ken first, as I was, according to him, a direct reflection of him and our ministry.

On January 19, 2010, I posted a piece about 1 Corinthians 14:40 and order in the church. Ken initially misunderstood the piece and felt like I was implying that I was criticizing the way we maintained control in our services. The piece read:

"The incessant hammering of control only drives a wedge deeper, separating leader from follower even more, creating even more distrust and discord."

"Honor equals order. Where there is honor, there is respect. Where there is honor and respect, there is love. And where all these things exist, there is order, because in a culture of honor, I am last, the people around me are first.

"In a culture of honor, there is no room for self promotion or personal gain. We minister to each other to build each other up, not to build ourselves up. And whenever there is need for gentle correction, a slight change in course, there is no room for offense, because there is honor."

The point I had been trying to relay was that control was unnecessary in a culture of honor, and thus I was expressing the pride I had in our church and the culture of honor we embraced.

Unfortunately, Pastor Ken was afraid that people might think I was implying that he was too controlling; his fear was realized when he reacted to it and attempted to control me.

He didn't make me take the blog post down, but I sure had some explaining to do.

The crazy thing is, I'd written about how the church was all about a culture of honor instead of control. Somehow the message had been twisted and Ken felt the need to use control to manage my behavior.

I became very agitated that Ken was trying to control me and the expression of my personal thoughts, especially because I hadn't intended to write anything to conflict with his viewpoint. Veronica tried to reveal the level of control Ken had on me, but I would have none of it.

"You are your own person," she said, trying to empower me. "You don't need his permission to express yourself!"

Even though I knew she was right, I couldn't bring myself to accept her words of wisdom and support. I'd dedicated myself to this man and convinced myself that I was called to serve him. I closed my eyes and blindly defended the man who was stifling my ability to ask questions and challenge the way things were, and in doing so, I stifled her too.

I would snap at her if she even implied that Ken had anything but the best of intentions for me and my family.

But if I was honest with myself, I was already growing uncomfortable with his influence and his intrusion into both my personal and spiritual life. I hated having to choose between staying true to myself and honoring the covenant I'd made to him.

It was the first time since making the covenant that there had been any attempts to bring me under control, but it would hardly be the last.

13

IMAGE IS EVERYTHING

Both Veronica and I liked the informal atmosphere at our Friday night gatherings. We both had a voice and a vision for it. Ken seemed less controlling and was respectful of the simple structure of food, family, simple singing, and talking as a group. This was the format we had proposed to him originally.

In the weeks following our ministry trip to Florida, Pastor Ken began to get it in his mind that we needed to move to Sunday mornings if we were going to be a "real" church. The church we'd ministered at in Lakeland had a large sanctuary, seating for about one thousand and state of the art sound, lighting, stage and video equipment.

When Ken started talking aggressively about changing our gatherings to Sunday mornings, about becoming a "real" church, Veronica suspected he'd been opposed to our vision of church all along.

"Don't you see?" she pleaded. "This is what he's always wanted, Travis."

"I can see what you're saying and why you think that," I replied, trying desperately to avoid the continuous conflict that pit the covenant relationship I had with Ken against the covenant relationship I had with my wife.

I knew that a Sunday morning service, a "legitimate" church, and a deeper budget—all of these things were enticing to Ken. But I'd dedicated myself to his service, so what could I do?

The covenant I'd made with Ken kept me in a state of constant conflict. Even though the vision was changing from the vision we once shared together, I hadn't committed to a specific vision; I'd committed to him.

Veronica wanted out, but she couldn't get out because I was in.

I was stuck in the middle, being forced to choose between the vision for church that I shared with Veronica, the one I'd thought Ken shared as well, and this new vision. For Veronica and me, the new vision was really just a return to the way of doing church as a performance, as a show on a stage—a stage we'd been chased from years before in the church we'd left.

Ken and I had several conversations about this, some heated. These conversations almost always came with the implied ultimatum that things would be done his way with or without people who disagreed with him, and so to maintain my influence in the ministry, I'd bend to support his vision.

Once again, I chose Ken over Veronica. She was mystified by the hold he had over me. After I informed her the decision had been made (behind closed doors by our all male board of directors) to make the move to Sunday mornings, she said with a scowl, "Good luck getting me to come." I knew she'd come around. After all, I was the head of the home.

I guess I didn't realize that by making such accommodations to my vision in order to support his own, I didn't really have any true influence on things at all. The golden handcuffs that came with the covenant ensured I would continue to tow the line.

I knew the decision to move our services to Sunday mornings was financially driven. Several of the regulars in attendance at our Friday or Saturday evening gatherings also attended other churches on Sunday mornings, so we knew it was likely they still tithed to those churches. Assuming we would attract them from their current Sunday morning place of worship, we'd be able to secure all of their financial support or at least get a clear understanding of who was really committed to our vision and who was not.

And so, in April 2010, we held our inaugural Sunday morning church gathering.

Veronica and I submitted to Ken's new vision, but for the first time as his followers, we found ourselves going against our own gut feelings in order to honor the covenant I'd made.

As we pulled up to the old movie theater with our musical gear in the back of the trailer on that first Sunday morning, both of us felt like we were going against our convictions. Simply starting another Sunday morning church service had never been part of the vision. We had been creating community, but this felt like we were becoming just like every other one of the hundred or so churches in our city.

The motivations for launching our Friday night gatherings had been pure, as we were seeking to create a community of Jesus' followers that would really do life together. Our vision was to create the type of relational "church" that you read about in the New Testament. We'd never intended to mimic the type of church that has become popular in western culture; from the beginning ours was meant to be different. The city we lived in hardly needed another Sunday morning church service, just another church adding to the clamor for people or their tithes.

Pastor Ken was now drawing a full-time pastor's salary, which was quite the financial burden to carry for our seventy or so congregants. When things got financially tight, he'd always threaten to get a job, but was clear that if he did, there would be no way he could do as much as he was doing in service to the church. In other words, if he did take a "tent-making job" to help support himself and his family, the church would suffer.

Though I didn't ever dare voice it, I wondered why Ken couldn't just get a job and minister on the side. I had a job and still found the energy and passion to give it my all in ministry. Our vision had been for none of us to "take" or draw from the ministry. Slowly this had changed, and I didn't like it. The purity of our original vision had become tainted, and this was the most glaring flaw.

On a regular basis, Pastor Ken would speak of everything he had left behind for the sake of the call. "When I was in business, I was easily making double what I make now, being your pastor," he would say just prior to taking the morning offering. Statements like this always made me feel bad for keeping him from success, as though we as a church were holding him back from reaching his true potential. I'm sure it worked on most of the members of our congregation, believing he was sacrificing for our benefit.

Veronica and I struggled with the move to Sunday mornings, with becoming a "real church." It felt as though our pure vision for ministry had become twisted and tarnished. It felt more real to us to have families gather together for a meal and join in worship one evening a week, engaging in conversation about our faith and growing together.

Though she objected to this departure from the original vision, Veronica served alongside me as always, but she was conflicted. It had been years since we'd led a band from a stage in a performance labeled "worship." After leaving our previous church, embarrassed and disgraced by judgments made, she'd sworn never to expose herself in such a vulnerable way again.

And yet, for me, she did it. She laid it all out there. The woman connected to God in a way I never would. For her, it was never about the words or the music; it was about the feeling. She could tangibly feel God. She wasn't leading worship; she was experiencing the divine presence of God.

Nonetheless, honoring the vision of the man to whom I'd pledged my life, I helped secure a rental deal at a local movie theater on Sunday mornings. I hoped that we could maintain the low-infrastructure, less-material church feel by renting a venue for our Sunday morning worship services. I was always hoping to keep the physical footprint smaller while creating a larger relational legacy.

From the first Sunday morning meeting in that movie theater, with the band set up in front of a sixty-foot screen, Pastor Ken was already looking for a permanent venue. We "needed" a space with classrooms for Sunday school, offices for staff members, and room to create new programs such as a supernatural training center.

Our original vision was definitely slipping away, with Veronica and secretly even me left wondering if perhaps our original vision had been just a means to achieve this end goal. Perhaps it always was about finding a career-making star vehicle for Pastor Ken.

Five weeks later, we signed a lease on a four thousand square foot building. There was a large, open space with twenty-five-foot ceilings where we could hold our gatherings. There were five additional rooms we could use as offices and classrooms.

Pastor Ken was over the moon. We'd finally made it! A real church in a real building, only two years after we'd launched our Friday evening meetings. Success.

I hadn't really imagined a scenario like this one, but because of my dedication to the man, I joined with him in his jubilation. It was at that point I finally gave in, letting go of the original vision. I couldn't fight it, so I might as well join it.

As an artist, I became distracted by the shiny objects we were purchasing to outfit our new space. We had to secure everything needed to create a first-class church-going experience. Sound equipment, video projectors, computers, stage lights, video cameras, and a custom engraved pulpit for Pastor Ken—no expense was spared. We decked out the stage, stopping just short of ordering fog machines, although we planned on adding those later. If we were going to do this, we were going to do it right. Tens of thousands of dollars was an investment for people's souls; at least, that's what the people were told.

When I think of it now, with an open mind, we were creating job security for Pastor Ken. The more we built in infrastructure to support him, the more secure his future could become. As a former missionary, Ken had a great fear of slow months, where there would not be enough income to cover expenses. I'm sure all those years on the mission field covering their own losses with personal savings was a contributing factor to the extravagant way we were spending donated money to create a framework that would basically guarantee enough recurring income to provide security for Pastor Ken and his family.

Having completely abandoned the original vision, I now dedicated myself to designing the lighting, sound, and video systems while simultaneously commissioning a flashy new website. We were creating a seamless and immersive multimedia church experience.

Everything revolved around the way we looked. As I led the team creating the image that we would present to the world, I remember saying, without flinching, "If we view this church from a strictly business perspective, this stage, this pulpit, is the product, the money-maker, and we have make it look good." At the time I felt none of the shame I feel now about that statement; now, I realize the clear commentary it provides as to the mind space we were in. I was empty.

~

By the time we launched our first Sunday morning in our new building, we had a camera crew live streaming our services to the world. Everything was as it should be except my heart.

In a matter of weeks, I'd made the transition from an honest, impassioned worship leader to someone entirely different. I'd become a producer, putting on a show. When I stepped on that stage Sunday after Sunday, at the top of my mind was how we looked and sounded. We'd been blessed with some incredible, studio-quality musicians, and I regret the missed opportunity to play music and create art simply as a beautiful expression of worship to God. Everything I did was driven by an agenda to become popular, to attract attention to the ministry and us.

And popular we became.

For the most part, Veronica and I were beloved by the people, a darling example of what a couple that is following their calling should look and act like. Everyone knew our names, and we felt famous, even if we were big fish in a small pond.

With the glory also came fire. While many praised us week after week, stroking our ego as worship leaders, a select few would consistently critique the worship each week. Nearly every Sunday after basking in multiple, ego-boosting compliments we would be subject to at least one complaint, ranging from sound levels to stage presence to song selection.

We took people's complaints very seriously; after all, if viewed strictly as a business then these were our paying customers. Like a professional sports team, we would "view the tapes" each week, noting areas of weakness in our performance and creating strategy for improvement.

Even though we always made the gesture of deflecting the praises we received week after week away from us and up towards God, we were definitely immersed in a culture that glorified worship leaders. We actually had fans. It was both surreal and intoxicating.

Pastor Ken had far more fame than we did. He had a following that extended far beyond our local congregation, or so he told us week after week. I think it was all part of his method of control, to make the people feel blessed to have such a well-known and loved pastor.

Everything we did was judged for the way it appeared through the lens of our high-definition video cameras. We were careful to shoot from angles that made the church appear much bigger than it was, never letting an empty row show.

Every once in a while, I would reminisce about our original vision. On one of the very rare Sundays we weren't leading worship, I remember sitting in the mezzanine and looking down over the congregation. I looked past the soundboard, the media computer, and the video mixer and gazed out at the people. It hadn't started this way. We'd started this community with the best of intentions. From the first meeting on a Friday night where the unique concept of our church was born, all kinds of great ideas were pledged. We'd be different. We'd rent space for our worship nights but let the rest be relational, meeting one with another. We planned a free-flowing, conversational, interactive expression of faith.

Once we became distracted from our vision and started paying salaries, setting operating budgets, and acquiring our building, we needed to maintain momentum and income to continue to function.

We were obsessed with our looks, constantly working the books and watching the bottom line. We knew if we couldn't get enough people to fill seats, then we couldn't make budget, and if we couldn't make budget, then "we'd just have to close the doors." At least, that's how we explained it to the people whom we knew had more to give.

It was fun at first, but after a while I knew we'd lost our way. Only the covenant with Pastor Ken was causing me to stay. The dream of only a year or so before was becoming a nightmare. I was lost.

Leading worship became routine. I knew what the people were expecting. They were starving for connection. The atmosphere we'd created left each member of our church "family" standing alone in a crowded room of worshippers, focused on the desire for "feeling" God.

I gave them what they were looking for.

I engineered our worship services to become the emotional experiences the people were looking for. I became adept at creating song sets, key changes and musical transitions that would leave our congregation in a mesmerized, trance-like state of reverent euphoria. Then I would let Pastor Ken handle the manipulation from there, often continuing to undergird his words with my music, continuing to draw on the emotion of our people.

Obviously, the people were still feeling something, as the church was still growing. Underneath it all, nothing was happening for me. In my heart, I felt absolutely no connection with God and had lost all sense of His presence.

14

CONTROL

The new vision for our church was slowing killing me. I felt a whole lot of silence and emptiness. Emotionally, I was cold, lonely and hollow. After six months of faking through worship and feeling guilty about going through the motions by performing for an audience, my physical body was starting to feel the weight of the internal emotional conflict. Lakeland was gone. The vision for community passionately connecting together in worship was gone. I was dying inside.

I was torn between maintaining personal integrity and living in honor of the man I was in covenant with and whom I had promised to serve for the rest of my life. The key words of our ministry at the time were truth, honor and integrity, so that made it even more frustrating. I was living a lie and had lost my integrity, yet I had done so for the purpose of maintaining honor.

How much more could I bend before breaking? How much more could I be controlled before I would finally crack?

Two weeks before the grand opening of our new church building and the launch of our Sunday morning services, we were working day and night to get everything ready. I worked my day job from six a.m. to six p.m., grab some fast food for Pastor Ken and myself, and head over to the church to meet him, continuing to work on the set-up and preparations for our big day. We usually worked until after midnight, hanging the LED lights, running cables, and testing the sound system; everything had to be just right.

We were working so hard to create a cutting-edge venue. One night, at about 11:30p.m., Ken slowly descended the ladder after hanging the last stage light, and we rejoiced that we'd completed one of the final tasks before our launch.

We both agreed it was time to take a break. We would get through the opening Sunday and then take a few days to rest and recharge. We found out there was a leadership conference taking place at one of our favorite churches in California, and we decided to leave on the Monday following our kickoff service and drive down.

The premier Sunday came and went off with out a hitch. We made it seem like we'd been doing this for years. The video was live-streamed online, and the service's official podcast was ready for download mere hours after we said our closing prayer. Perfection.

Exhausted from the weeks of planning and prep work, I headed home to spend a couple of hours with Veronica and the girls, since I hadn't seen them much over the previous twelve to fourteen days. I had already booked the early part of the next week off from work, so Pastor Ken and I agreed to meet the following morning and head out on our mini-road trip, in dire need to clear our heads and rest. I had high expectations to reconnect as friends, as we'd been pretty driven lately, our conversations terse and "to do list"-related.

For the first few hours we reveled in our accomplishments, congratulating each other for the hard work and generally just celebrating the events of the weeks leading up to the successful launch of our Sunday morning services.

As the white-dotted lines of Interstate 5 flew by, Pastor Ken asked me about how Veronica was doing, given that I'd been pretty much an absentee husband of late. I told him part of the truth, that she was a little stressed and definitely needing some more time with me, and the girls missed their dad. As a husband and father himself, I knew he would understand. At least, I hoped he would.

What I didn't tell him was that much of what was causing Veronica to be stressed out was our fairly sudden departure from our original vision of a unique gathering of Jesus people who would join together as family. For all intents and purposes, we now had very little to distinguish our new little church from the more than one hundred other churches in the city.

I did, however, mention in passing that Veronica was dealing with her stress by working out at our local gym and taking up yoga.

I was about to be forced into a conversation of control like none we'd had before. Due entirely to the fact that the passenger seat which I occupied was located less than three feet from the driver's seat where Pastor Ken sat, I had relinquished control of both the conversation and the vehicle.

"Yoga is a cult," my friend and mentor said. "You can't let her get into that stuff."

I tensed up. Control had become a regular part of our relationship, and I was preparing for the worst. Of course, I still had a ton of respect for this man, so even though he seemed to be crossing a line in the conversation into my personal life, I was compelled by our covenant to hear him out.

I relaxed my grip on the leather seat I'd been squeezing like one of those stress balls and responded to Pastor Ken's concern about Veronica taking yoga classes.

He'd begun his criticism of Veronica's choice of fitness activities in a fairly patient, gentle way but slowly worked up to what would become an ultimatum.

For the remaining seven hours of our drive, we talked about yoga, even though if we were both being honest which each other, neither of us possessed adequate knowledge on the topic. Nonetheless, by the time we reached our hotel that night, he'd broken me. I repented for failing to protect my wife from her own ignorance.

He continued to tell me just what would happen to her if she opened her mind to the dangerous religion of yoga. Even though I tried to make him prove how a certain sequence of stretches at our local gym could possibly cause her to turn and pledge allegiance to the Evil One, he insisted I forbid her from taking even one more class.

The moment we arrived at the hotel in California, Ken insisted I call her immediately and inform her as her husband and spiritual leader that she would not be allowed to return to the yoga studio.

I called her let her know that she would not be needing the lululemon pants I so loved seeing her wear, and she might as well leave her baby blue yoga mat at the curb with the rest of the trash. The conversation did not go well. She already felt like I had given too much control to Pastor Ken, and this was going too far. I had initially hoped I wouldn't have to tell Veronica about the ultimatum my pastor, mentor, spiritual father had delivered, but I finally had to tell her: it was the popular fitness activity or our position on the leadership team. That was it. Were she to continue to engage in the dark art of yoga, she and I would both be forced to resign as associate pastors of our growing church.

It didn't make things any easier, but after a while, and under protest, she knew she would have to submit to me as her husband and spiritual leader in the same way I had submitted to Pastor Ken.

Pastor Ken would eventually allow me to let her take kickboxing at a local Christian-run club after researching that they wouldn't be teaching her any pagan martial arts techniques.

Yoga was the first issue Pastor Ken had actually been able to fully control—not that he hadn't tried to interfere before or that he wouldn't try again in the future.

~

Another area in which our personal freedoms had been limited or at least scrutinized was permissibility of the consumption of alcohol. It was not permissible. Ever.

For most of the years we were in relationship with Ken and Diane, alcohol was simply not a topic of conversation. Yes, we knew of "Christians" who consumed alcohol, but the dangerous road of "social drinking" was one we were not going to travel. We were taking the high road, the "highway of holiness," Pastor Ken's go-to term when describing our code of conduct. It was basically a way we could distinguish ourselves from the small "c" Christians, those lackadaisical believers who weren't true enough to the cause of Christ to allow his message to truly affect their way of life.

Veronica and I enjoyed wine for the majority of our married life. So, even though I'd revealed nearly every corner of my life to Pastor Ken, this secret remained. It was the pioneering belief I held that differed from my mentors. It was probably the gateway belief, the single piece of independent thought that would give me the confidence to challenge everything in a revolution of thought revision that would be at the root of the shattered relational covenant between Pastor Ken and me.

While Ken and Diane were out of the country ministering for months at a time, we had no need to hide our freedom, but whenever they were in the same town, both Veronica and I feared our secret would be discovered. As we grew into more confident adults, we feared less but still joked about it, scaring each other into thinking pastor Ken had just walked into the restaurant and was about to discover the glass of Pinot Gris on the table next to my filet mignon.

More than once, Veronica successfully fooled me into believing the secret was out, and I'd conceal my glass under the table while verifying her claim. Of course, she'd be laughing uncontrollably at that point while I gulped the glass of chilled white wine in attempt to cool my flushed face and calm my nerves.

Alcohol was also the only prohibition lifted in our time together. "Social drinking," a term I abhorred when he used it, became acceptable to Pastor Ken years after I'd been secretly partaking of alcoholic beverages with Veronica in the privacy of our own home or on romantic dinners.

The ironic thing was how my pastor and mentor was indirectly responsible for a significant increase in the expansion of my own personal drinking habits. On one of my late night airport pickups, retrieving Pastor Ken after an out-of-town ministry trip, he started talking about how the leadership of the church at which he had been speaking had a much more relaxed policy on drinking. I could tell he was gauging my reaction.

"Oh really?" I replied, truly interested in the intended direction of the conversation. I hoped for nothing more than to be able to cease the cover-up of my consumption of local wines.

After hearing that he had not joined in the celebration of freedom as the host church's leaders had, on the flight home he did request a rum & Coke. I hid my surprise. I still hadn't determined if he was repenting and this was some sort of accountability partner thing or if we were about to hit the nearest bar and get wasted.

Indeed, we hit the nearest bar & grille, and we grabbed a bite to eat. We walked into the restaurant and were seated in dark corner, at a thick, well-worn oak table. I waited with bated breath as the waitress read us the specials and then asked that life-altering question:

"What can I get you guys to drink?" Even her tone of voice had changed, the inflection becoming deeper, alluding to the forbidden.

"I'll have a double rum & Coke, in a tall glass," he said with confidence. Then, looking at me, he added, "You want one?" For a man who "didn't drink," ordering a double rum & Coke was an auspicious beginning.

I played it cool and answered with a nod, as if I'd ordered liquor-laden beverages before. The fact is, the entire repertoire of alcoholic beverages that I'd ever consumed contained only two items: red and white wines.

From that point on, things changed yet again. You see, Pastor Ken and I now had our own secret, and eventually we would share this secret with Veronica. I am not really sure if Diane ever knew, or perhaps she did and wished it weren't so.

Veronica and I went from sneaking a glass of wine only when we were out of town, so as not to cause any of our congregants to stumble, to stocking a full liquor cabinet in our home at Ken's suggestion. Only weeks after having our first drink together on the way home from the airport, I was now spending thirty to forty dollars on drinks at each of our meetings. I paid for them, since Ken and I both knew alcohol wouldn't be acceptable on his expense reports to the ministry.

Ken suggested I just purchase the liquor we needed, and we could enjoy our drinks in our home before or after our regular ministry meetings.

I learned to mix several of Pastor Ken's favorite drinks, including the one burned in our memories from the thousands of times we'd heard his testimony over the years: A double Harvey Wallbanger. It was the drink of choice he gave up to go into ministry, and I'd become an expert at floating the Galliano over two shots of vodka mixed with orange juice.

Alcohol had become the relationship booster Pastor Ken and I had needed. His tendency to control me had been pushing me away, but drinking together began to change the dynamic. I have no idea if the members of our congregation noticed the change, but as far as I'm concerned, we definitely became closer after that first drink.

We were more than co-pastors; we were now drinking buddies.

15

COVERING

As our church plant made the transition from our original vision of spontaneous relational gatherings to a rigid, organized, pre-planned weekly production, we began to grow quite rapidly. Our balance sheet looked strong. So strong, in fact, that our board actually authorized a raise for Pastor Ken.

He had been looking to buy a new home in the area and was setting his sights on the high-end subdivisions set in the mountains overlooking our city. Our pastor was always looking for the best. He bought the best phones, the best computers, and the best vehicles and was now looking at a nearly fifty-five hundred square foot mansion on the mountain, complete with a one-hundred-eighty-degree view of the city below.

Appearances were very important to Ken. Much to Veronica's chagrin, he sold the car we'd given them and used the profits buy a better one. When I asked about his buying a new car so soon, he explained how important it was for the pastor to have a nice car parked out front.

If the pastor and leadership drove nice cars, wore nice clothes and had good jobs, then other people who drove nice cars, wore nice clothes and had good jobs would be attracted to attend our church.

This was another one of those cultish, kingdom-contrary moments I missed while enamored with all that was wonderful about Pastor Ken. He'd all but said we preferred the wealthy to the down-and-out.

The ugly truth was further expressed when we sought a location for our gatherings. It was important to Ken that we not locate too close to the areas of the city where the homeless congregated, making the same "mistake" that a sister church had made. While he believed some congregations were well-suited for that type of ministry, we were not one of them.

Because of his obsession with high-quality, expensive things, I found myself competing in a game of bigger and better. He would buy a new car, so I would buy a new car. He bought a new Ford F-350, and suddenly I wasn't as satisfied with the truck I had, even though it was only two years old.

On and on it went. Veronica and I learned an important lesson through it all. We realized we didn't want to be obsessed with material things. It was consuming us, and it was not healthy. So we sold much of our unneeded "stuff," including our own three thousand square foot home in the suburbs, and moved our little family of four into a two bedroom condo that was two thousand square feet smaller than our previous home.

It was another one of the small but independent decisions we made on our own, doing what was best for our own family. We had felt like we were being consumed in the competition for the biggest and the best. We wanted to give more of our finances to the church, and that meant reducing our mortgage and letting go of some of our possessions.

Not surprisingly, it really was a freeing experience. We've continued to pursue a more minimalist life when it comes to the things we own and the purchases we make. We've learned to be thankful for what we have, and we've found and enjoyed great value in the peace this perspective has brought into our lives.

Meanwhile, as we were simplifying our lives, Pastor Ken and his family were getting ready to move into his nearly three-quarters of a million dollar home. It was autumn, and I remember walking through this beautiful house for the first time and being amazed. It was gorgeous. And wouldn't you know it, there was a basement suite built into this house on the cliff that had the same one-hundred-eighty-degree view as the two main floors above it.

While touring the suite located at the ground floor of their beautiful mansion, Veronica made a surprise announcement. She wanted to leave the small condo we'd moved into only a year earlier and move into Ken and Diane's.

Years later, Veronica would tell me why she made such a rash proposal that day. She had realized she would never have all of me and was willing to make this dramatic change to be closer to me.

And so, after spending only one Christmas in our condo, we were moving in with Ken and Diane. We'd been under their spiritual covering for years; it was time to move in and become part of the family. We worked out a rental agreement and moved that November to the basement suite two floors below their living room, shortly after they moved in.

Veronica was so excited, as was I. Church business was taking up nearly all of my time after work, so being close to the people we were serving only made sense. We could do some of our meetings at the house, and we'd be spending more time with our friends as family.

I know I should have been more honest with Veronica beforehand about the doubts and fears I had about moving under their physical covering in addition to the spiritual covering they already held over us. Our freedoms had already been significantly limited already, so why would I choose to move closer to the source of the control? At least we could more easily invite Pastor Ken down for drinks, and no one would have to drive home "buzzed," as he called it.

~

The significance of covering was ingrained in us from a young age, specifically when it came to church membership and ministry. To me it always clearly presented itself with the similarities to a multi-level marketing company or based on a pyramid scheme.

The ladder of succession I personally climbed during my rise to prominence on the local ministry stage was from the bottom up. It starts with youth group. A young person volunteers and submits to a youth sponsor or leader, who in turn is covered by the youth pastor. That youth pastor is usually submitted to an associate pastor, who is under the covering of the senior leader. Sometimes, the buck stops here, but in certain Christian traditions, there can be several more levels to hierarchy.

When I was sixteen, on the first ministry venture I led on my own, the covering slogan at the bottom of the poster read: "The Daniel Project is an outreach project of The Brother's Embrace which is a ministry of Encounter Church operating under the auspices of International Outreach of the World (I've changed the ministries' names, but our covering was equally convoluted). It sure was a mouthful, but at least we had all of our ducks standing in a carefully covered row. "Who are you covered by?" or "Under whose umbrella are you ministering?" were common questions in ministry circles, and I assume they still are.

I always wanted to challenge Pastor Ken on his own covering claims, because, since we were so close, I knew his claim of being accountable to the pastors of that loosely affiliated ministry in California we'd recently visited was pretty bogus. In fact, the one time he did ask one of these apostolic super-pastors for advice about his plans to start a new church in our city, they actually shut him down, saying in their opinion our city didn't need another splinter group church, and we should unite with one of the other likeminded churches.

Of course, that didn't stop Ken. I think I was one of the only people who knew we were "outside of the covering" that he claimed to be accountable to.

In communities that hold the concept of covering, there always seems to be an apostle in the mix. I'm not sure how many pastors have to submit to the person's leadership or how many churches he has to oversee before promotion to apostle, but one thing is certain: Pastor Ken was an apostle. He told me so himself. Pastor Ken needed to be at the highest rung of every ladder. Maybe once he claimed the title of apostle then he believed additional covering was optional.

A wise man once told me, "If you have to tell people that you are an apostle (or prophet, evangelist, preacher or teacher), then you probably aren't one, or at least not a very good one."

The whole covering thing just sounds like a recipe for cover-up. To me, a system like this is just begging for things to be swept under rugs.

Covering was basically a method used to maintain control. I literally lost track of the good people we kicked out from under our covering, leaving them alone to fend for themselves out in a big, dark, scary world.

We spent just over eight months with them before things started to unravel and the fabric that held us together began to fray. It was last straw time. Control and covering had had their way with us for too long. We weren't afraid of that big, dark, scary world out there, even though we had no idea the emotional trauma we were about to endure as a result of standing up on our own two feet.

We were about to throw off the covering and run naked through the streets.

16

CRACKS IN THE WALL

About that time, in a rare expression of independent thought via the blog I still published, I wrote about what I believed the church was really about:

> *"Church can't be just another part of our compartmentalized lives...this many hours allotted for work, this many for school, a few hours for church... The Church isn't an event or a building. It is the relational community of the lovers of God, collectively known as Jesus' bride. In other words, the Church is about people living in unity with one another, forgiving differences, looking past conflicts... becoming one..."*

I'm sure if it were possible to track back to where it all went wrong, it was probably this scandalous train of thought, or one similar, that was a root cause. Maybe Pastor Ken read it and couldn't reconcile it with the direction he was taking our church. Maybe he didn't read it but could sense the openness, the freedom and the unconditional acceptance that was beginning to escape through my pores.

Our conversations towards the end were generally fairly impassioned as I'd present challenging questions and identify issues with the way things were being done in our church. Specific hot topics included leadership and ownership, the validity of our hierarchical leadership structure and our tendency towards performance-based worship.

The worship thing became a major point of contention in my own heart, as I'd always found peace in the purity of playing music and singing songs of freedom and forgiveness. As the years passed, we'd left the natural, organic, relational expression of our faith and transitioned to this institutional version of time limits, song selection, volume management, and the general church sanctuary dynamic. My heart couldn't have been further from the songs we sang each week on the stage that bound my feet.

I grew to hate having the music I played and the words I sang twisted and used to deliver a message that seemed in complete opposition to the conviction of my heart.

There were times I wanted to follow up one of Ken's words with a contradictory word of my own. We played one service in which we sang of grace, delivering a message of the love and acceptance of Jesus no matter where we are as people, no matter what we've done or what we're going to do. We sang "He loves us" over and over again, letting the divine love of God bring healing to our broken hearts.

Pastor Ken often interjected in a lull of a song. We were accustomed to "tag-teaming" throughout the service. As I continued to play, eyes closed as we basked in the aura of the acceptance and the love of God, my ears were assaulted with a violent call to repentance.

Ken was calling everyone who'd just been reassured of the unconditional love of our Father God that unless they quit sinning, they could never experience the love of which we were singing. This was the way he tied everything back to the theme Veronica and I had been singing of. His violent diatribe of repentance continued as he called anyone on the bumpy road of sin and death to make the climb up to the highway of holiness.

Then, and only then, could the people be one with God and experience his love. His formal message continued to further this fundamentalist agenda. He continued to preach of the separation between man and God, specifically calling out the sins of homosexuality and anyone engaged in premarital sex. These were his pet sinners. He was obsessed with them.

My disillusionment with this man and our mission intensified that day.

It was incredibly hard to sing about peace, joy and love from a stage on which a message of discrimination, judgment and even hate would be delivered only minutes after I stepped off. In my heart, I believed in a God of acceptance, forgiveness, peace and justice; and while officially those words appeared on our statement of faith on a wall in the church office, they were rarely spoken aloud in the words of a sermon.

As people who have spent literally thousands of hours combining the artistry of music with the poetic beauty of the Bible, many of us who once led worship in churches experienced a thrilling encounter with the good that is the ideology of the kingdom of heaven Jesus spoke of.

I couldn't reconcile the message of the man I'd committed to serve for the rest of my life with the message of Jesus.

Week after week, we would experience such intimacy with eyes closed and the music playing, but the moment we opened our eyes... it was gone, and what would happen next on the Sunday morning agenda would have nothing to do with what we saw in the kingdom of heaven.

And then I realized God is bigger than I thought.

When I finally awoke to the understanding that I'd been an accomplice to the abandonment of my own original vision, I realized we had become isolated, having no tangible, sensory experience with people anymore. We'd become atmosphere, an opening act warming up the crowd for the headline experience.

Our messages didn't even match anymore.

~

About six months prior, I had been pressured into accepting a very small, token "salary" to acknowledge the extensive list of tasks I performed in addition to the duties associated with our role as worship pastors. Everything we did was as volunteers and with servants' hearts, and we always donated much more to the ministry than we received back anyway. I think the money was there to make me feel valued and also as a way to keep me bound to the ministry.

It worked for a while. But my integrity eventually reemerged, having lain dormant for nearly a year as I sleepwalked through the motions, a castrated man, stripped of limitless passion for God by the confining and judgmental message of the man I loved as a father.

Everything was about to unravel. Little did we know, we were about to have one of our final leadership-related ministry conversations.

I received Ken's call just as I pulled into the driveway we shared, arriving home from work after six on a Friday night. His truck wasn't in the driveway, and I was tempted to ignore the call. I was getting ready to take Veronica out for a date, since most of our time together lately was spent serving at the church. I didn't want to kill the mood for our night together.

My devotion got the better of me, and I picked up the phone. He was still at the church, preparing for his message on Sunday, and had found himself reading through the founding documents of our non-profit organization.

He was calling to propose that we draft a change to our ministry's constitution, inserting a clause ensuring that the board could never terminate his position in the ministry. I was used to getting crazy requests from the leader I'd finally begun to admit was controlling and manipulative, but this one woke me up. "Wake up, O sleeper."

It was one of those moments where you wait for the punch line that doesn't come, because an absurd demand like that can't possibly be for real. Somehow I deferred my response to his request and suggested we take up the issue at our meeting the following Monday.

The light-hearted mood I'd worked to employ going into my first date with Veronica in months was completely destroyed. There would only be one topic of conversation during our night together. I knew it was time for me to try to release myself from this man.

Veronica and I decided together that we could no longer accept the money he'd begun giving us through the ministry. We felt like we were being bought. We didn't feel like leaving the ministry completely; we just wanted to step back and get a better look at what was going on around us.

The following Monday, when I made the request to Pastor Ken that I no longer wished to be paid for the ministry work I do, his first reaction was that he wouldn't be able to hold such high expectations of me. Incredulous, he actually said, "How will I get you to do everything I need you to do?" It was an ironic but telling comment.

His question revealed exactly what Veronica and I had feared. We'd let things degrade way past honor and partnership. I had become a (poorly) paid personality to provide credibility to the man and his ministry. Taking back our independence meant the hold he had on me was loosening.

~

As people, we'd been used and abused. We weren't part of a family; we were just another cog in the institution's machine—a machine we had helped to build. When we were finally able to wrap our minds around the fact that it wouldn't stop until we were fully burnt out, fully consumed, we spoke up. We stood up for ourselves and requested a much needed break, a rest from the weekly, even daily, grind of service in the church.

It was time to take a smaller role.

Included in my workload was the weekly maintenance of our website and blog posts, our weekly email update, the formatting and printing of the Sunday bulletin, the administration of our social media presence, editing the video from our weekly service, filming episodes for our online show...the list went on and on.

We didn't leave anybody hanging. Both of us remained open to leading worship, while Veronica offered to continue to serve with the women's ministry, and I was willing to continue to perform the duties of a board member.

I had by no means released myself of my ties to Pastor Ken, either. In an email listing the responsibilities we were relinquishing, we included this statement:

> "We remain committed to keeping this church our home church family and we remain committed to the covenant made: that we have your back, we stand behind you and will defend you personally, your family and this ministry in honor."

The strained response we received from our "friends" Ken and Diane was manipulative, engineered to display love and understanding, but their disdain and disapproval stained through.

> ...both Diane and I are disappointed...

...Travis, I have never really known you in the capacity you are moving into, so it will for sure be some major adjustments for us all...

...Probably the saddest part for me will be missing the "time" we spend together while talking vision for the future, and having you as some of my closest friends... I know we will still be friends, but things usually do change when such a radical shift happens...

The limits of our relationship were being tested. We'd never found ourselves in a position like this before. I hated the passive-aggressive way he suggested our friendship would change as a result of my decision to relinquish some responsibility in the ministry. It was his way to keep me tied to the work we were doing.

Our friendship and his mentorship had started long before we founded the church we had become consumed by. That he would use it for leverage hurt my heart.

Veronica and I both hoped for a chance at a restart. Things were bent, not broken—or so we thought. We were completely unaware that we were less than five weeks away from complete relational failure.

17

AND EVERYTHING CHANGED

The shift changed everything. It had been about a week since we'd talked. We'd traded emails back and forth about my requested change in duties and responsibilities, but once he had used friendship as a bargaining chip I sort of shut down. I had not imagined this possibility. All of the scenarios I had run through in my head had positive endings, with acceptance and understanding at the center.

Things were getting a little awkward. We'd never found ourselves in a place where we disagreed and I didn't simply acquiesce. Since the covenant, I'd simply been conditioned to agree with whatever my "spiritual father" asked me to agree to.

Standing at the tailgate of my Dodge pickup truck, which was parked in the shared driveway in front of Pastor Ken's home, I was loading a variety of sporting equipment, bikes, etc., preparing for a long weekend away with my family. A much needed Sunday off. Now relieved of our weekly administrative duties, I knew this was our chance to reflect on where we'd been, where we were heading and whether we needed a change in direction.

I heard the front door of the house open and close and then footsteps approaching.

"I think this is the longest we've ever been apart," Pastor Ken said, breaking the ice from behind my left shoulder. I was lifting the two-inch ball hitch and receiver into place and was reaching for the bike rack when he began to speak again.

"I need to get a sense of where you are at, Travis," he said.

As he spoke, I watched his reflection in the chrome bumper of my truck. I would have been much happier to pack for our trip without having an awkward conversation. It was moments like this that I regretted my decision to move in to his basement.

"Where I'm at? I'm right here. I'm the same," I began, reverting to a self-preservation strategy of hiding my true emotions. Obviously, I was not the same. Theologically, we were heading in very different directions, though neither of us was bold enough to admit it.

All of a sudden I heard some words leave my mouth that caught me by surprise, too late to retract: "It's not like we're gonna leave the church."

"Whoa, I had no idea you were thinking of leaving!" He seemed genuinely shocked. To be honest, so was I.

It had been a long time since I'd expressed any independent thought out loud He'd imposed strict parameters over the content I released to my blog for at least a year. I rarely explored what I believed anymore. In that moment, I realized I had a near primal need to check in with myself at the earliest opportunity. My own words were surprising to me as I spoke them; things had reached a critical warning level.

I began to shiver; my hands shook. I held on to the tailgate of my truck for support, trying not to let him see the physical toll my body was taking as a result of being honest and standing up for myself. Leave the church? How could I even think of it? We'd poured heart and soul into this thing since we founded it together nearly three years earlier!

I took a deep breath, turned my back and lifted the bike rack into place, continuing, "I guess I just need some room to breathe, figure a few things out."

He was not impressed. He asked for a meeting before we left that evening to come to an understanding, but I declined. I remember being aware that putting off the meeting he had requested until returning from our weekend away would have dire consequences, but I didn't care.

I needed some time for myself. I'd given Ken such a high level of honor that I hadn't reserved any honor for what was going on inside of me. I made a decision to stand up for my own health, both physically and mentally. I was quickly realizing that if I were to take the meeting he'd requested, I would be too weak to stand up to his mind games.

I couldn't leave town fast enough.

I hurriedly finished loading up the truck, and the kids, Veronica and I left for the long weekend. The four-hour drive was integral as we explored our thoughts, feelings and theological beliefs.

Before we left I sent Ken a quick message on behalf of Veronica and me:

> *We understand that this is a trying time, and we are being slow to speak while we process. Things are becoming clearer for us and we will have a more definitive response to the unanswered questions soon. In Jesus' Love, Travis*

What we discovered on our mini road trip would lead us on a journey that would change our lives forever. Veronica and I finally talked about the hours I had been spending away from her, serving the church. Even in the weeks prior to my awkward conversation with Pastor Ken in the front yard, I'd been at the church nearly four hours every night after work. I was starting to miss out on important family time. Our girls needed a dad, not a pastor.

Without exaggeration, this conversation is one of the only talks I can recall having with Veronica during the entire time we were working to build the church with Ken and Diane. I expressed a deep sorrow for abandoning her. That day, I embarked on a long road of repentance to win back her heart.

We'd always been empowered as a couple to minister together, and Ken and Diane's children had been great babysitters, making it easy for Veronica to minister with me. In the months preceding, babysitting had been less available, and thus Veronica would have to stay home with the kids while I continued without her.

I'd forced her to make the sacrifices I was willing to make. I'd rarely consulted with her along the way. When it wasn't possible for Veronica to minister with me, I'd barely acknowledged her needs and pressed on alone.

As we drove out of town to spend a long weekend with family, we reconnected in a very special way. Veronica cried as she shared the pain in her heart that we were being torn apart. A couple of weeks earlier Pastor Ken had told us both there was a time his wife Diane had to step out of public ministry and take care of their children. He didn't go as far as to say that Veronica do the same and take care of our own children while allowing me to freely come and go in ministry, but he did put it out there. At the time it had gone over my head as a conversational anecdote, but the message was not lost on my wife.

It seemed like for Pastor Ken, my wife and girls should come second, but to me they came first. I never did get a clear understanding of his priority list. I know his own personal list would sometimes bring ministry and God together, equating them and justifying the making of ministry a higher priority over family. This didn't work for me.

Although this is something I had never meant to do, I knew I had done it; I'd followed Ken so closely and been so deeply immersed in ministry I missed the warning signs reminding me that my family was suffering. Not only that, I was suffering. Physically, I wasn't healthy; mentally, I was strained; and spiritually, I was cold and isolated.

Standing up for myself and my family was a big step. Reducing my workload at the church to spend more time with them had gone a long way to show Veronica that my family came first. When the time came for me to choose to continue to minister alone while my wife stayed home with the kids, the choice was crystal clear. It was time for me to exercise my independence from the man I'd served and loved for so many years.

I knew I was at risk of breaking the covenant I'd made years before, and even though I feared the threatened consequences, we returned home from our weekend away to commence with a month of meetings that would mark the beginning of the end of our lives in the public eye of ministry with our dear friends Ken and Diane.

18

DARKNESS FALLING

Upon returning to town, I retrieved several voicemail messages from Pastor Ken that had been left for us while we were away. The first of the messages carried a softer, gentler tone than the more urgently worded "Call me as soon as you are back in town!" message that completed the trilogy of recordings.

We were rested, recuperated and ready for whatever was about to happen. The meeting I had declined to take before leaving for the weekend away as a family was now overdue.

I set up the meeting as requested, inviting the couple who we still thought of as our pastors and best friends over for tea that same evening. Ken and Diane felt an urgency in their spirits to connect with us and see just what was causing the tension we were all feeling.

That evening, our lion-maned pastor and his wife sat down with us in our basement suite for a tough conversation that was in a sense a prequel to the disastrous meeting that would occur two floors up just over three weeks later.

Ken and Diane made themselves comfortable in our small living room. Our conversation began peaceably enough. They talked about how much they loved and cared about us and how sad they were that we would be taking a break from active ministry.

Things had begun to change, as all of us could agree. I challenged Ken on the vision for ministry and church we'd created together years earlier. He admitted things had naturally progressed to a place neither of us could have anticipated.

As I continued to press Ken as to whether he felt we were following our own original intentions, I realized though none of this was what I had intended, it fit him like a glove. It had given him a security he'd never had, and I knew he liked it.

It occurred to me that the only people who weren't fitting in were Veronica and I.

The people we led together, in a church now consistently drawing over one hundred people each week, needed to see unified leadership, or so Pastor Ken said. I was still stuck on why that meant we should simply close our mouths and follow him.

I was struggling against the man whose ministry I'd helped build. Years of mindless submission had removed my voice from the equation. I became aware of how replaceable I was. Ken didn't need me anymore; the church was more or less self sustaining.

In the beginning, Ken had been extremely accommodating to our vision, as it served his. Now, however, with all of the major components in place to continue the operation of a successful church, there was no need to make concessions to my own vision.

Finally, I pressed him on the issues he spoke against with such vitriol and on which we fundamentally disagreed, letting them fly in rapid succession:

"How can we as a church hate gays?"

"Why are our doors closed to the people who need this the most?"

"Why are we obsessed with sin and not the grace of God?"

"What are we even doing!?"

It was another of those moments where my own words surprised me. I thought to myself, almost amused at my own boldness, "Shit just got real."

I didn't receive a clear response to any of my questions. Ken attempted a weak semblance of response about how we don't hate gays; we hate their "lifestyle." We'd welcome them in our church as long as they weren't actively engaging in sin.

It wasn't about the answers that weren't coming. The questions weren't even the point. I didn't expect to find common ground on these issues. These were just the questions I hadn't dared to ask until now.

When it became apparent we were on a path that was clearly different from the path of the church we were serving in and that we wouldn't easily make our way back to the well-trodden way acceptable to the most senior leaders, a final Hail Mary play was attempted—a kind of a last ditch effort to regain our compliance.

We had been talking for at least a couple of hours. The sun had set beyond our balcony on the edge of the world, and even then I remember thinking to myself that I would miss this place. Early on in the conversation, I'd resigned myself to the worst possible outcome. Once I got real, sharing from my heart, I knew there was no way we could come together.

The outcome had been inevitable. If not that month, then next. If not that year, then another. The covenant I'd made had caused me to hide who I was out of honor for Ken. It was an impossible situation.

I'd made it very clear just how vast the divide was that separated us. I knew I'd caught him off guard. Based on experience, I knew the conversation wasn't about to improve.

His voice deepened, and he got much more serious.

"Travis, this separation isn't meant to happen," he began, taking a stern, somber tone. "I really can't tell you what I see over you right now," he continued, referring to the invisible supernatural world that he alone could see in the room. I'd seen him to do this routine before many times, but I was shocked he was trying it on me.

I almost said, "you've got to be kidding me," but I stayed quiet. Over the years, through all of his supernatural, angelic visions and visitations, I'm sure he noticed I had never seen a thing. Not one angel, not one demon, not one "orb." I had felt we were beyond this type of manipulation, but I suppose at this late juncture he was willing to try anything.

He had honed his "seeing" gift into a well-practiced craft. He'd made an art of using the unseen to affect the seen. This is the creepiest thing about our time in a church that walked and talked like a cult, this tendency to "look" into the invisible—the supernatural—and use it to affect reality. How easy it seemed for my friend to cause people to believe after creating a supernatural reason they couldn't.

"I can't tell you what I see in the supernatural right now, but it saddens me deeply," he said with an air of superiority. He continued, "A prophet should only release ten percent of what he sees, and I see something over you that is very hard to take."

At his words, Veronica jumped to her feet and challenged him on making a statement like that. Her arms waved around as she took him to task on the controlling, power-wielding action of withholding his vision of the supernatural to manipulate the moment.

"Oh no, you don't," she yelled fiercely in my defense. "You don't get to come in here and do 'that' to my husband. You better tell us what you 'see.'"

Finally he relented, saying it was against his desire, but he would share what he "saw" over me.

Ken stood in our doorway with Diane tucked slightly behind him, his eyes closed and brow furrowed. Veronica stood between them and where I still sat on the couch.

"I see a dark being in the supernatural, a darkness over Travis," he said, likening what he "saw" to an angel of death. Continuing to prophesy, he declared the hand of God and His favor would be removed from my life and my business would suffer because as we stepped out from under the covering of the ministry we had co-founded together; I'd be left exposed.

What's ironic was that Ken couldn't see the real darkness in my life, the one he had helped create. It was a complete loss of integrity that had come at the expense of my covenant with him. He was too blinded to see that his spiritual manipulation of me had literally killed my desire for church, or at least the kind we had been practicing. I was in darkness, but he was the oppressor.

Ken went so far as to imply that they could sense "darkness" seeping into their home through the floor and vents.

Veronica immediately and vehemently denounced the "vision."

"This is bullshit!" she began. "We don't accept or receive this!" She made it clear that we weren't buying into their claims that we were a source of darkness in their home. We didn't accept what he'd told us he "saw" or the word he delivered to accompany the vision.

I rose, stunned, while Veronica aggressively showed our Pastor and his wife to the door before slamming and locking it and finally slumping into the sofa beside me.

Dazed, my emotional energy exhausted, I thanked her. She stepped in to stop Ken's control and manipulation. In the same way she'd once thanked me for saving her from her controlling father, she was now saving me.

We were making too many waves with our desire to engage with, minister to, and help people in an organic way instead of simply performing for them. That night's conversation had been a last ditch, manipulative effort to get us back in line.

After that meeting, I am sure it was understood we were a lost cause.

In the lonely days that followed, we wrote a song called "Chase The Dark Away" with the intention to bring peace back into our hearts and home.

To anyone who has ever wondered,

"Who am I and what have I done?"

To everyone who can't remember

How you got here or where you came from...

Let lights shine around you and chase the dark away

Let heaven break open and light stream down...

If you've let your past become your future,

The bright lights have faded and you've disappeared

Though shadows surround, you can't hide forever,

Let life and let love conquer your fears

Let lights shine around you and chase the dark away

Let heaven break open and light stream down...

On that very dark night made darker by the controlling, manipulative words of my mentor, Veronica and I held each other closely, believing the light of God's love would soon shine through.

It's always darkest before the dawn.

19

HOPE...IS LOST

A few days had passed since Pastor Ken felt it necessary to reveal the dark side of my soul, at least from his vantage point and ability to see into the supernatural.

People had begun to realize there was trouble in paradise, and murmurs and rumors were now being spread throughout the ministry. Once they'd grown to a dull roar, something had to happen. I was called before the board, a group of five guys which included my dad, three close church friends and Pastor Ken.

Veronica was not invited, nor was she welcome at this meeting. It was time for the men to talk. That's how you can tell when something is super serious in the evangelical stream of Christian churches: when the males gather to discuss a matter, you know it's a big deal.

I arrived fashionably late for this emergency meeting at which I was the sole item on the agenda. The tables had been turned on me as I sat opposite the five members. I felt like I was about to pay for all of the times I'd sat with our board and removed people from their positions of ministry because we had determined that they had sin in their lives or had failed our impossibly high expectations in some other way.

I walked through the door of a building that had literally felt like a second home to me. As I descended the stairs towards the basement offices, I had an eerie feeling this would be the last time I would ever set foot in a place that now held so many bittersweet memories.

I peeked in the door tentatively before walking into Ken's office. Each member of the board looked at me with sadness in their eyes and hugged me before we began. When I hugged Ken I made sure it felt non-committal and empty. He'd deeply hurt me with the whole angel of death thing.

The hug was reciprocated in a similar manner. Much love had been lost between us over the last couple of weeks.

For an hour or so, Ken spoke without really stopping for air. He talked of the good times and thanked me for my service, but then he began to tear into my record of offences. I was "charged" with insubordination; he felt I was challenging his leadership and questioning his decisions. He spent an inordinate amount of time criticizing blog posts I'd written which he'd determined demonstrated a perspective different than that of the ministry

Basically he was trying to throw me under the bus for occasionally thinking independent thoughts. As we'd determined a couple of days earlier in our basement suite, I had more than a few ideas that did indeed run contrary to the thoughts of Pastor Ken.

Things weren't going well for me. How I longed for Veronica. As this meeting was an office meeting of the board of directors (all male), she wasn't permitted to attend.

And then, a surprise.

When it came time for each member of the board to respond, they stood up for me—affirming me, protecting me and caring for me. They took the opportunity to discuss my unique perspective, goals, vision, dreams and needs. Suddenly, things were looking much better. These men I counted as friends had come through! They were extremely accommodating and had made my future a few shades brighter. Pastor Ken even seemed to turn his disapproving gaze into a somewhat hopeful expression.

When I left the meeting, I felt significantly lighter, as though a heavy weight had been lifted from my shoulders. I walked through the door at home to share with Veronica dramatically more positive news than I had expected.

The church was going to honor our request to step out of most of the administrative duties but was adamant that we still be encouraged to lead worship whenever we felt like we were able to. Special arrangements were made for us to have at least two weeks off per month, and the option to lead worship without a band for a while, if that's what we needed to do in order to return to our roots. I could even write whatever I needed to write.

It was an amazing feeling. One of the board members even invited Veronica, our girls and me over to their home for dinner the following night.

We arrived at Luke and Rachel's with our girls just before 6:30. We'd been surprised by the invitation, as most of the leaders had been avoiding us like the plague since news of the tension between Pastor Ken and I had gotten out. Since we got along pretty well with this couple, and it seemed like they were just reaching out, we agreed. They served us an amazing meal of ribs, corn, and potato salad. The works. We were so spoiled.

Luke had joined the board of directors about a year earlier, and both he and his wife were great encouragers and cheerleaders of our ministry. The church had also recently named them elders because of the way they cared for people. They had done wonderful things for our family, filling our children's room with toys their daughter no longer needed, helping us renovate the suite we lived in at our Pastor's home, and just loving us as their own.

When we left that night, Veronica and I talked about how loved we felt and how we felt Jesus' love through those two people. We'd had a wonderful evening, laughed a lot, and really didn't talk about the struggles we were sorting through.

Things were truly looking up. It was great to have a personal, relational night out with someone who knew of what was going on but just wanted to show love regardless of the circumstances.

~

By noon the very next day, however, things took a turn for the worse. I received a call from my dad, one of the board members, who was very concerned about my "behavior" the previous night. For a moment, I racked my brain to try putting any meaning to his words.

"What are you talking about?" I asked.

"Last night at dinner," began my Father. "I heard you had your arms crossed the whole time and didn't want to talk about anything. Why were you being such a jerk?"

I was completely caught off guard. How could this information have been spread and misinterpreted so quickly? It had only been twelve hours since we'd left the Elder's home, flooded with peace and love in our hearts. Somebody had been busy.

I tried to imagine how I'd been construed as a jerk the previous evening. Had I said or done anything that could have been taken this way? Were my arms crossed the whole time, and if they were, should that matter? The questions were still swirling as I tried to answer.

"Man, I don't know what to say," I told him. "We spent most of the evening telling stories to each other about our kids! I laughed so hard my stomach hurt."

"Well, what's with your arms being crossed the whole time?" he asked.

Incredulous, I strained to remember if my body language could have portrayed even the slightest negative vibe. And even more so, I was at a loss at how information from our dinner the night before had so quickly been transmitted from our gracious hosts to Pastor Ken and then to my dad.

"It was cold out, and we were on the patio until late in the evening," I replied, wondering how it could possibly matter.

As the conversation continued, my thoughts raced. Why would they have reported to the board about our evening together? Why was this all so political? Was I so naive to think we could have a meal together without my words and actions reported back to mission command?

Our "friends" had taken the information they'd gathered during our dinner, and apparently our body language as well, back to Pastor Ken. Like undercover secret agents, we were lulled into a false sense of security, and then they turned us in, throwing the book at us.

Little did we know when we sat down for dinner that fateful night that we'd be betrayed by morning. And wouldn't you know it, those were the best homemade BBQ ribs I've ever had.

We received an email from Ken the same afternoon requesting our presence for an emergency meeting to be held that very evening in their home, two stories above ours. Officially, the meeting had been called because apparently I hadn't sufficiently communicated enough with Pastor Ken since the board stepped in and expressed their acceptance of me just the way I was.

Veronica and I had actually expected a very different outcome on that infamous evening. As strained as things were, we had seemed to be finding some common ground, first with the board of directors and then with the head elder couple, Luke and Rachel, at dinner in their home (before we'd discovered they'd reported back to Pastor Ken).

Notwithstanding the recent body-language setback, Veronica had a positive outlook about the meeting to be held that night. My outlook ranged between doubtful and cynical.

We arrived five minutes earlier than the scheduled start time. All of the other invited guests were already seated in Ken and Diane's living room. I looked around. My dad sat slightly out of the circle, on a chair he'd grabbed from the dining room table. We shared a look that made me feel like I'd let him down. I hated the feeling I was bringing my drama into his life. I knew he was there to support Veronica and me, but if there are two things my dad doesn't do well, conflict and drama would be the top contenders.

I glanced at the heating vents near the couch as I sat. There was no seepage of darkness from our suite two floors below. The meeting commenced in the same way the board of directors meeting had begun in Ken's office, only this time, the people who'd stood up in my support weren't in attendance.

All of the special accommodations that had been made at the previous meeting were taken off the table. Veronica's hopes of breakthrough based on the commonality of our faith in Jesus were dashed. Though the stated intent of the meeting was to bring closure and emotional healing, our hearts were broken and our dreams for the future crushed.

We'd been called before the church leaders and were stripped of our title, position, responsibilities and home. To this day, we remember that night as one of the worst of our lives.

I remember looking across the room at the couple who had served us an amazing dinner paired with loving, non-judgmental conversation and just asking, "Why?" Luke had looked back at me with Judas' regret and tears in his eyes while Rachel looked away, and said, "Travis, I'm sorry."

It was over.

20

FINDING MY VOICE

Everything we'd ever known or believed about God had been called into question. We were homeless. We were heartbroken and had lost all hope.

Finding a home was a formality. In three days, with the help of my family, we were moved into a temporary space and were making plans for something permanent within the month.

Finding hope was a foregone impossibility. Our hearts were numbed with pain, disillusionment and betrayal.

We had a hard time trusting anyone. We isolated ourselves from everyone and everything. My family helped provide some stability, but we were still on our own with this. We knew they were talking about us, but who could blame them?

Veronica's family was initially supportive, but would eventually turn their backs on us, effectively excommunicating me. Veronica and the girls were free to have a relationship with them, but they would have nothing to do with me.

Not willing to compromise our love, Veronica chose to separate from her family. Losing them would prove to be far more heartbreaking. Hers is a story I hope to tell someday, but that time has not yet come.

In a world that had turned cold, dark and ugly, I started to look for ways to find beauty again. I was seeing shades of grey and needed to inject some color into my life again.

I found what I was looking for in a local art teacher, Donna Senft. It was under her caring eye that I learned to paint with watercolors. Twice a week for six months I returned to her studio for three hours at a time, letting the colors run from the paper into my soul. There is a beautiful sunflower hanging in our home as a result of my artistic pursuits.

I had to lay down my paintbrushes to finish this book, but I look forward to returning to this peaceful expression of beauty. "Miss Donna" is currently passing on the love of art to my daughter, Tehillah.

Veronica found solace and expression in the form of a community choir for a season. We sought peace.

For six months, our Sunday mornings were silent. We had a lot of extra time. We'd found a place to call home, even a dream home, and I'd been given a big promotion at work. Overall, we were happy and healthy and whole.

So, not dead. Not living outside of the favor of God. Not surrounded by a cloud of thick darkness or whatever Pastor Ken had said he "saw" over me in the supernatural.

Life was actually good and getting better.

I had begun writing again, writing some of the pieces that would eventually become this book.

Out of the blue, on a particularly dark and stormy November afternoon, I received a phone call from Pastor Ken. I answered, but only because my curiosity would have killed me had I not. He wanted to get together for coffee. Completely caught off guard, I agreed to meet him that evening.

We reminisced for a while. He relayed stories from the church, and I told him about the book I was writing. I even told him I was writing and promoting it under the working title Churchburned. I openly but respectfully expressed my disagreement with the way we had "done church." He actually thanked me for not really creating too many waves when we "left." I didn't feel the need clarify that we'd actually been pushed out, and rather forcefully at that. Why fight? He could read about it later in my book.

I was keeping my cool and engaging in mature, rational conversation with a man whom I'd once deeply loved.

When he inadvertently spoke of manipulating people on his ministry team who weren't cutting it, I physically felt my temperature rise. He spoke of people who weren't giving it their all, and if I'd learned one thing during my term serving Pastor Ken, if you weren't for him and his ministry, you were against him.

For much of the conversation until this point, I hadn't really looked at him. As I listened to him tell stories of control that were eerily similar to the one we'd been engaged in less than a year earlier, I made a point to match his gaze.

I looked deep into his eyes, the same eyes I'd looked deeply into before committing my life to him. His eyes told a story that differed significantly from the one he spoke aloud.

He'd aged a lot since I'd last seen him. There were new wrinkles gathered around the outside edges of his eyes, and deeper creases in his forehead. He looked tired. For a moment, my heart ached for him. I was starting to believe he'd simply gotten caught up in a broken system. I began to feel compassion for the man.

I don't even think he realized how cold and calculated it sounded as he spoke of the people who'd taken my place in the ministry. To him it wasn't manipulation; it was people management. I used to use the same verbiage when I was on the inside, justifying our in-game actions by pointing to the score at the end.

Nearly six months had gone by since we'd been forced to resign. It was truly with great heartache that Veronica and I had delivered our letters of resignation to the board. It was the second hardest letter I have ever composed in my life. The hardest one was yet to be written.

We never could have imagined writing a letter of resignation when our community of passionate followers of the way of Jesus first began meeting together all those years ago:

> *When Veronica and I began serving in our current role, the atmosphere was intimate and organic, and we were blessed to be a part of a ministry that fit who we are. It was the informal, family-like culture that drew us together. As the church has grown, a bureaucratic system of leadership has been instituted to manage the ministry, and we've found ourselves unable to thrive under the more formalized structure. Our personal style of leadership and*

outlook on church expression is different than that held by the leadership.

Our family is our most important priority, and we will tenaciously pursue God's best for each one of us, even if it looks different than expected from the outside looking in.

Over the last two years, we have grown and matured in many ways, and we will always hold this church family close to our hearts. We are grateful for the freedom we had to express our worship to God, and for the many exciting experiences that we had along the way.

We wish only the best for you as you continue to lead the church, and we believe for abundant blessing over His church.

Their letter of response had been less than gracious. Our now former pastor and his wife blamed us for causing unrest and a lack of peace in their home due the fact that I was "breaking my verbal covenant" with Pastor Ken. Their letter also explained that we were being evicted so they could be at a place of peace and continue to pursue their calling. Their response was signed "with all our love." It was impossible to believe that.

After a rather short but civil one hour and fifteen minute coffee date, we hugged goodbye, both of us realizing we'd probably never cross paths in a ministry-type situation again. We were going in completely separate directions.

We had not actually addressed the covenant that night, in our final coffee date, but to say it was the elephant in the room would be an understatement. It had been in a Starbucks much like this one in which I'd made a covenant and pledged to serve this man for the rest of my life. I know it was at the top of my mind throughout the meeting; I highly doubt it slipped his.

I did still carry a great deal of guilt over the covenant. I was raised to be a man of my word. I wrestled with terminating the life-long commitment I'd made at the wise age of twenty-five for several weeks before I did finally work up the courage to break it.

Veronica and our girls were simply more important to me even if choosing them over church meant God was going to remove his hand of favor from our lives as Pastor Ken had prophesied. I don't believe for a second God did or would remove his hand of favor from our lives.

We intentionally endeavored to seek love and peace all the more since experiencing the most dramatic shift of our adult lives. We'd chosen to fan the flames of love instead of letting hate creep in. We surrounded ourselves in love, thus ensuring that God surrounded us.

The final meeting with Ken proved the ties he'd bound me with were finally broken.

It was time to take back my life. It was time to empower my own destiny.

21

BREAKING THE COVENANT

As much I'd like to have believed the ties had been broken between Ken and me, there was still work to be done.

How was I to know at the age of twenty-five that making a covenant to serve a man and his ministry for the rest of my life was wrong? I had been conditioned for that moment for years. I'd been raised to believe that people who left the church had bitterness issues or sin in their lives. But now I was that person. Even though we were fluent in the principles of the kingdom of heaven, as taught by Jesus, I was going through hell inside.

We began to hear stories from people who we'd once been close to as ministry partners and as friends. The words we'd been told Pastor Ken had been spreading about us were hurtful lies. Rumors spread about how we'd left the church because our marriage was on the rocks or because we'd become alcoholics.

It was heartbreaking to hear toxic words had continued to bleed out of their mouths long after our departure. That we were still emotionally affected by the rumors helped reveal more work would have to be done to release ourselves from the covenant I'd made.

One story attributed to our pastor was that during a secret, random inspection of our suite he couldn't even walk through without crushing empty beer cans under his feet. We didn't even drink beer. If anything, he would probably have been tripping over our children's toys as he snuck through our connecting door.

I began to see a counselor who helped me understand that even though I used all the right words, my actions proved I was actually not following God even though I was still convinced I was. It was during these therapy sessions that I was able to identify what I would need to participate in my own restoration.

I discovered that my faith had been in Pastor Ken, not God; my life had been informed by Pastor Ken's love, not the love of God. When he was disappointed, my god was disappointed. When he didn't show love, my god didn't show love. I had made him my idol, and I was worshipping him by serving him, by dedicating my life to him. I received my validation from Pastor Ken and the attention he gave me, praising me in both public and private. He stroked my pride and thus guaranteed my lifelong loyalty.

I was living in a reality far removed from the reality Jesus spoke about. We'd bragged about the covenant I'd made to him; we'd showed it off so others might follow our example. In truth, the covenant was grotesque.

After several months of therapy, I finally believed the covenant I'd made with Pastor Ken was wrong. Late one Monday night, I sat at our kitchen table and wrote down the words I'd pledged years earlier on a piece of notepaper.

"I'm here to serve you, to see you flourish. I will never leave. I will serve your vision for the rest of my life."

I hated those words now more than I meant them way back then.

When I made the covenant, I believed I was laying down my life to serve another, and I believed I was following a trustworthy leader in the example of Jesus himself.

The process of separation and the ensuing therapy helped reveal what I'd truly done by making a covenant to this man. I'd broken, or at best threatened, the lifelong commitment I'd made to Veronica on our wedding day. I'd become distracted from the simple call of love, the simple experience of grace.

When I'd initially broken the covenant with Ken, the conflict with Veronica became apparent immediately. It was like I hadn't really honored our bond for years. She barely held half my heart. In the years since and the years to come, I've committed to pursuing love with her.

I abandoned the potential and talents God has given me and replaced them with the pursuit and creation of a replica of the kingdom of heaven. Stepping back, I was able to see that I didn't have to help build the kingdom of God on earth. Learning to live as a follower of Jesus helped me discover that the kingdom of heaven is all around us, should we choose to live there.

I carried the notepaper with the words of the broken covenant around with me for a week, stopping every now and then to read them and remind me of the way I had bound myself to a man, of the way I'd created this disgusting wall between me and God. Every day I contemplated those sick, twisted words until I eventually couldn't even look at the paper without feeling nauseated.

At the end of the week, I prayed to God, alone and together with Veronica.

I repented.

Then I took the paper I had been carrying in my pocket for the previous seven days and lit it on fire. I burnt the covenant that had held me captive to Ken. It was a symbolic act meant to end the covenant.

I was rising up, for the first time rejecting fear and believing in my heart God had forgiven me and still loved me. That was actually the easy part. The hard part was forgiving myself and telling myself that I loved me, that I was proud of me.

In my heart I knew I was worth it, even though I'd conditioned my mind to be selfless. Somehow, instinctually I was learning to love myself, which is a key piece of learning to love one's neighbor as one's self as Jesus taught.

I doubt any of my neighbors wanted to share a piece of my self-loathing. It was finally time to rise above the condemnation. It was time to hold on to my dignity, undefined by the story, and experience the truth. It was time to confront my deepest fears.

~

I nearly got sucked back into the drama and the lies shortly thereafter when I read through an email Pastor Ken had sent to church leadership but that had also been copied to me. It nearly killed me to read the hateful, passive-aggressive message, composed and delivered even after meeting for coffee and hugging goodbye only a month previous.

In ministry or any form of life, you will always come across people that just don't seem to like you or the Church. Or they have been hurt...usually by their own issues, but you or the Church seem to be the brunt of their assault.

When I read on the Internet such things about the bride of Christ, the church, or leadership ... some even trying to "burn" the Church, my heart goes out to them.

It is such a terrible thing when a disgruntled person feels the need to try to justify their bad choices by trying to convince other sheep to join their cause of "hurt" or "church burn."

My blog at the time was called "Churchburned.com" and my audience were the unchurched, overchurched, and spiritually manipulated. I hated having to read his reference to me. The rest of the email was even harder to read, as he carefully crafted his words to insinuate that I'd blasphemed the Holy Spirit, something he had taught in sermons as the only unforgivable sin. As such, the words that followed basically condemned me to hell.

When I read them for the first time I literally collapsed to the floor, heartbroken.

...just because you messed up as a leader or member, does not give you the right to "blaspheme" or lie about what the Lord and Holy Spirit have built and are doing in the church and peoples lives...

...You have a problem with church, Grow up and GET OVER IT...

...Does it give you the right to throw the baby out with the dirty bath water?? NO. Chances are... you might be some of the dirty water...

The heartbreak turned to furious anger then rage, and my initial reaction was to post a damning response on my blog, calling out the calloused, non-Christian act. Fortunately, probably as a result of our dedication to the way of love and peace, I waited. Sure enough, as the anger died down I was able to feel compassion and empathy for the man who felt it necessary to write such hurtful words about me.

The very same night, after reading and rereading his vindictive letter, I began drafting a letter of forgiveness to Pastor Ken, a letter that would also serve as my declaration of freedom. It was time to for redemption. For the better part of a year I'd brought condemnation on myself for breaking a covenant I knew to be wrong, but I was only now releasing myself from my own judgment.

22

BROTHERS, ESTRANGED

As hard as our letter of resignation had been to write, our hearts breaking with every word of it, the letter of forgiveness and declaration of freedom was the single most difficult letter I would ever deliver in my life.

I spent several days writing the handwritten letter on the best stationary I could find, selecting my finest pen. This letter was written with intention. Several times, I crumpled it and started again. Once I finally signed my name, I carried it around with me for two months before I actually found the courage to send it.

The reason this letter was so difficult to write was because it meant letting go. There would be no one left to blame. It meant letting go of the pain, letting go of the past and allowing my story to be redeemed.

March 6, 2012

Dear Pastor Ken,

It's been nearly a year since we parted ways. When I look back, my memories are bittersweet. I thank God for the time we had together, but I regret not maintaining honesty and personal integrity throughout the last two years. I should have been open and upfront about my personal beliefs about church and the way we were doing things long before our relationship flew apart. For this I am sorry.

I know I broke our covenant. I was no longer able to accept its validity as through personal growth I learned to believe that I wasn't to be bound to a man. I'm sorry for the pain I caused you by breaking that bond. I hope that we can begin to replace it with a bond of peace and unity in Jesus.

I hope that you know that in reaching out to the hurting, to the misfits, to the unchurched and the over churched I've never meant to hurt you or anyone I've been in relationship with. I strongly believe something is broken with the way we do and have done church, that's all. We'll likely never agree on this, I assume.

I know there have been times where I've come across too strong or appeared less than loving, and I'm working on that.

I became offended by some of the things I heard second-hand, about what was being said about us, and how others were being hurt. I now hold forgiveness and grace in my heart for anything I've held against you, as I really don't know whether these things were said or done in the same way they were relayed to me.

Over the course of the last few months, God has been leading me to seek reconciliation and forgiveness. I've been learning that the heart of our Father is restoration and redemption. We may never see eye to eye on a lot of things, but we are still followers of Jesus and thus brothers.

As a brother, I come to you and repent of the things I've done to cause you pain and confusion. I felt trapped and unable to truly express myself or truly be me.

I pray that the Lord continues to work in and through you, as He always has. Perhaps you will be more fulfilled as you transition into the next phase of ministry. I know your heart has always been for the church worldwide, I hope beyond hope that you will have opportunity to thrive in the coming years.

In Jesus' relentless love and overwhelming forgiveness,

Travis

With that letter, I released him forever. Peace began to trickle in the day I physically placed the letter in a mailbox. About a week later, I received an email thanking and acknowledging the receipt of my handwritten letter. The email contained his usual ramble but was signed with a most painful accusation:

> *I am deeply saddened at all the "damage" to other relationships that has transpired through this last season. Intentional damage to the Bride of Christ is a terribly huge responsibility.*

I read it several times, initially hurt by the judgment he had rendered with a sharp jab. I pondered a response. My body began to feel weak, and I felt like caving in.

In response to my letter of peace, he'd actually fired back. In his usual passive-aggressive style, he was implying I was causing intentional damage to the church.

Then it happened.

I began to reject the judgment, becoming confident of my innocence. I was free from his disparaging words, free of the manipulation and oppression I'd subjected myself to for all those years of faithful service.

There was nothing that bound me to accept the judgment he was making about me. Hell, there was nothing that bound me to even read it. Had I still been constrained by the terms of the covenant I'd made to him, Ken's latest accusation would have wounded me, and I would have been forced to take whatever vitriolic abuse he could muster.

But now, I was feeling something amazing: freedom.

The realization of freedom brought me to my knees as peace flooded my soul.

23

PEACE, JOY, LOVE

We have a saying in our home which comes from the Bible, "Let peace be your guide." When it comes to living life, just being human, loving the friends and family who stood with us, and forgiving those who turned their backs, there truly is an incomprehensible, overwhelming sense of peace that cradles us as we embrace each day.

When I think back to that dark evening in June 2011, when our hearts were broken and we lost our best friends, our church and our home all on the same night, there is a peace that surrounds my thoughts. To be completely fair, even though the four people sitting across from us that night seemed comfortable acting as judge, jury, and potential executioners, I bet they were probably just as stunned and distressed as we were that we were having such a conversation. Well, that may be too gracious. Other than Veronica, no one else found refuge in the restroom, throwing up and physically expressing the emotional pain, but I'm sure it had to be hard for each of them to do what they felt they had to do.

At least I believe it was.

Looking back, one of my biggest regrets of becoming enamored by ministry is missing those moments with the love of my life. Nothing is more important to me now then living and loving "in the moment." It's become an "if we speak with the tongues of men and angels, but have not love" kind of thing for me.

I'd love to tell you every step we take is an intentional step of vision and passion, unhindered by the things that once held us in submission, but if I told you that, I'd be lying. Sometimes our pace is purposeful and determined, and sometimes we're just having fun. Sometimes we stumble and fall, and sometimes we believe we can fly.

We had stood up for ourselves and allowed ourselves to be exiled in an act of self-preservation. Once we realized we had been duped into following a façade of the faith, any semblance of peace was evacuated from our hearts.

We'd rather be on the outside of the illusory faith in which we were participating then to continue to experience a counterfeit kingdom of heaven for even one more day. Nowadays, it is extremely rare to think of ourselves as being on the outside, as being rejected, because the institution and the people operating it who gave the impression they were the top of all that matters were wrong. There's so much "out here" we were missing while we hid "in there."

For my family and me, specifically for my wife and me, we felt like the pain of losing our church family and then much of her family was too much to bear. There were times when we didn't know how we were going to make it.

Over the past few years, a peaceful forgiveness has slowly filled the empty parts of my heart. Where I'd previously made and maintained space for the sole purpose of holding on to painful memories, the precious, divine love of God eventually consumed and filled me. Ever so slowly, the pain began to numb as we pursued forgiveness in our hearts.

As we walked alone, we experienced times of great, unexplainable peace, and then we felt like questioning everything we'd done and said since separating from the religious establishment that had nearly suffocated us.

As we learned to forgive, peace held us tightly and taught us to love. We were being drawn back into redemption. If leaving and taking my family into hiding took courage, then coming out was one of the most courageous things I've ever done.

When peace replaced fear and love replaced duty and belief, joy began to sneak up on us again. Unspeakable joy. Mischievous joy.

~

When I began writing this story, I didn't know how it would end; we were still very much on the journey. I guess in a sense, we still are, sojourning through life but with a different perspective. When I began to write, I had not yet found a resolve to the conflict that began this painful, exhausting yet beautifully rewarding journey.

That's changed now. When I speak of mischievous joy, I mean it. Over the past few years, we've had the opportunity to do some of the "don'ts" and break some of the rules. After a while we realized that we had been living in fear and denial. Inside the controlling regime we knew as church, we were careful to follow clear rules, maintain healthy boundaries with worldly things and live "biblically."

During a band rehearsal back in the peak of our ministry careers, I remember talking my team through an exercise, the purpose of which was to imagine heaven. It was one of the first times I started going "off-script" with our band devotionals. Instead of preparing and teaching from a selection of Scripture and encouraging change through the conviction of the words we read, I wanted to try a more multi-sensory, tangible experience. We climbed to the top of a local mountain and sat in a row, looking down over a meadow with a powerful river cutting through it.

We had about thirty minutes until the sun would set. We sat or lay on the slightly moist grass at the top of the hill on that chilly fall night. We gazed across the valley, and as the light show in the sky began, we allowed ourselves to imagine heaven.

Let me clarify something.

We came from a particularly charismatic Christian culture that was comfortable with visions, dreams and prophetic words. Books about people who had been taken to heaven and been given personal guided tours of specific rooms in God's castle were popular. There would always be a message. One minister wrote about being taken to the treasury and discovering that the coffers were low. He was very successful in raising revenue for his particular ministry, preaching a variation of the "whatever is loosed on earth is loosed in heaven" message, so giving more of our money on earth would also fill up the storehouses of heaven. Many of us soaked that stuff up. Me, not so much.

This was not the experience I was aiming for in this particular night. I had asked my friends and band mates to use their God-given "imaginations" and dream. I remember sharing my own imagined vision of heaven. I pictured myself walking to the river below us and diving in, discovering I could breathe under the water. I still remember the clarity of the dream. I remember sharing it with such joy.

I knew it was imagined; I had intended it to be, but there was so much childlike faith expressed during our shared, agenda-less experience. Each of them had their own beautiful dreams to share.

I didn't help draw connections between our heaven dreams and the way we should live our lives here on earth. Nor did I help find a correlating scripture verse for each person's experience. I did, however, help connect the dots between the unlimited beauty and greatness of our imaginations and the God who created us to dream.

When the rules of religion are removed, our experiences with God are truly limitless, and it is these limitless, unrestricted experiences that will change the world.

When we choose to love rather than hate, when we choose to accept instead of judge, this is when the divine spirit of God is honored. The kingdom of God is truly at hand when we forgive, when we create, when we restore, when we give, when we care, when we love.

At the heart of my faith in God is a belief that God is love. I don't believe God can be without love or that there is love in this world without God.

There is a verse in the bible, found in 1 John 4:16, and it reads, "God is love. Whoever lives in love lives in God, and God in them."

Discovering the love of God has been my favorite part of this journey.

24

GRACE

In the three years that have passed since "leaving the church," I've come to an entirely different understanding of the inaccuracy and insignificance of that statement. If the church is an institution, then yes, I have indeed "left the building." If the church is limited to a group of people who meet on Sunday mornings, sing songs and listen to someone talk, then yes, it would be hard to fit my actions into that specific box.

But I have discovered that there is space for all of us in the kingdom of heaven. Jesus demonstrated the way of peace and surprising, irrational love time and time again. So much of the healing and recovery from years of manipulation, control and spiritual abuse came through the realization that I am accepted by God because I was created by God.

I do not have to change in order to receive approval. I am the way I am because I am. Because God intended. Because Jesus redeemed. There is no striving to be good, to be better, to gain the love and grace of God.

I've had two liminal experiences that have helped shape my recovery and journey towards authenticity in myself and my faith. Both experiences occurred under the roof of a Christian institution; one was filled with love, grace and acceptance, and the other was bathed in condemnation and judgement.

~

In the first, I'd decided to sign up for the Faith and Culture Writers conference before I realized there would be worship at each of the main sessions. Traffic had been bad through Seattle on my way down from Vancouver, BC, Canada, to Portland, Oregon, so I'd missed the worship part of the evening session the night before.

It was the first time I'd been in a worship service since leading my last one over three years earlier and walking away from my church that same Sunday.

Here I stood, amongst hundreds of writers whom I've grown to respect and even love, and I was ugly-crying through the worship service.

I found myself standing in the dead center of a church sanctuary; eyes clenched shut while tears streamed down my face. My lower lip was quivering like a bowl of jello in the hands of a toddler. My hands were shoved deeply into the pockets of my Levis while my body seemed to shudder and be moved by every word that was sung.

There was no hiding it. With every word lifted towards heaven by the artists surrounding me, the tears of release came even harder. These people and the God we were singing of were healing my soul.

I had this overwhelming feeling that each one of the singing voices was singing over me, that every word uttered was being carried by the melody across my face before making its way to heaven.

Or maybe this was heaven. I was lost, wherever we were.

When the talented worship leader had begun to play on her piano and exhort us to join in worship, I bristled, bracing myself for the flood of negative emotion and criticism about to ravage my mind.

As she sang the words "…and together we sing," I didn't join in. But I did close my eyes. I imagined leading at least a thousand worship services just like this one over my fifteen years as a worship leader. All of the pain of leaving church and all of the negative emotions related to it were ready to take me down.

I considered bailing on the conference and walking out, but the voices singing in unison all around me soothed me, calming my racing heart.

These weren't members of the hierarchical leadership from the toxic, cult-like, fundamental, charismatic "church" wherein I'd experienced my dramatic rise to prominence and subsequent fall from grace.

These weren't the people who had hurt me. This choir of voices that stood all around me were the same voices I'd followed on my journey away from the place of toxic faith. These were the prophets who were willing to question everything, to write vulnerably and publically and let their lives lead mine.

That's when my lower lip began to quiver, and I felt my eyes well up with tears.

That's right, the big-bearded guy in the middle of the room began to cry, and it wasn't pretty. The tears flowed down my face, through my beard to wet my shirt. I began to sniffle and snort and possibly even whimper. Fortunately, the music was still playing and the people still singing.

So many of these people had gone through similarly painful church journeys and were finding their way back to an understanding of who they were and what the church was and how the two fit together.

Such peace and healing filled the room. What an amazing feeling to discover God in this way. A divine love and acceptance. It felt like we were making space for each other, regardless of the way we chose to see the church. I was accepting them as brothers and sisters, and I felt accepted by them.

It was like finding relief as I revealed the fear, the pain, the memories of my soul to the very type of building and the very same type of people to whom I attributed it.

~

The second experience was basically the polar opposite.

I only felt a hint of uneasiness as we walked into the building in which we'd spent most of our childhood attending church and school.

Even though we'd "left" the church, we'd continued to keep our daughters enrolled in a children's Bible course held on Thursdays after school. This was the very church we'd attended from birth until leaving in dramatic fashion after being laid bare on stage in the most memorable worship service of our lives.

Both Veronica and I had gone through the course as kids, and since we were uncertain about our future involvement in the church as we once knew it, we felt it would be a good idea that our girls get a basic introductory education to the Bible. The format was supposedly void of denominational theologies and was a simple, Bible-based curriculum.

Watching our girls sing their songs, recite their Bible verses and receive their diplomas filled my heart with joy. Veronica and I reminisced about our childhood experiences of attending the same Thursday afternoon children's Bible course as kids and learning about God and the Bible from the very same woman who was teaching our girls.

The initial uneasiness made way for a peaceful feeling as I realized that even though we aren't "church-goers," we were accepted as we were. Some of the people there knew our story and were kind, including a former pastor who made a point to stop and sit with us in our row near the back before the event began, making small talk and just being human with us. It was nice. I was feeling safe.

And then it was time for the woman to deliver her message to the parents and grandparents who were there to take photos of their little Bible scholars as they walked down the aisle in cap and gown.

The woman, someone whom we'd always loved and respected, began speaking of the reason she'd dedicated so much of her life to the "indoctrination" of our young people. She spoke of the dangers this generation faces and how there are people who call themselves Christians who are starting to question whether all of the Bible was directly inspired by God.

Ouch! There it was. My uneasy feeling was back. I shifted in my seat near the back row of the auditorium as I leaned over to Veronica and said, "I'm pretty sure she's literally speaking about me."

Perhaps the woman had read my blog, then called "Churchburned," or perhaps someone had tipped her off to my "backslidenness."

She spoke of others who've been deceived into believing evolution and dangerous humanist curriculum being forced on our children in public schools. She said "public schools" with a disdain you would only recognize if you were educated in a Christian school.

The evening drew to a close, and before we gathered up our girls to leave, we wanted to thank the teacher and take a moment to reminisce with her of our time in her course nearly a quarter century earlier as six and seven year olds ourselves.

Later, I would come to regret the decision to engage her in conversation.

As we approached, she seemed weirdly uncomfortable. Veronica sensed what was up. The woman, who'd taught both us and our girls the basics about the Bible, knew. She knew we weren't going to church anymore. She knew we weren't "leading worship" anymore.

And then it came. God was supposedly about to "speak through her." This is something people in charismatic circles like to pretend they can do.

She told us she'd heard from God, and she had to be obedient to deliver his message for us. She said, speaking for God, "you've gone off-track just like many other former worship-leading couples have." She looked at me and told me, "Even though you may feel 'enlightened,' you are actually deceived by the one who comes as an angel of light."

There was no resolution to her message. She basically delivered it and walked away. Yes, she told us she was delivering her message in love. We were left stunned, standing in a crowded room yet feeling completely isolated. I wanted to run as fast as I could. We scrambled to gather the girls' special Bibles and made a break for the car.

Spiritual abuse and manipulation hurts. We returned home keeping our smiles on for the girls and their "big night," but this one really hurt.

I think she was trying to pull me, one of the lost ones, back into the fold. It was kind of counterintuitive, though, given that her method of manipulation caused us to run away from the church we were standing in together as fast as possible.

We headed home with our daughters with an almost identical feeling to the one we'd had after leaving the infamous worship service. Dread. Pain. We wondered again, "God, why didn't you protect us?"

And then it happened. We didn't rush the girls off to their rooms, collapsing on the couch under the intense emotional pain. Veronica and I smiled knowingly at each other, a familiar peace filling our hearts. Then we laughed. It was a deep laughter, a joy springing up from within the depths of us. A new confidence was building in us, at the soul level.

The next morning, I sent the woman who delivered her "warning word from God" a bouquet of flowers, with this message: Thank you for teaching our daughters about God. Just so you know, we are passionately following Jesus, embracing His love, grace and peace and rejecting fear.

It's true. We are. And it's good.

~

These two experiences, my most recent interactions with the church in an organized, traditional expression, have helped distinguish the difference between the divine peace, joy and love of God and the religion I once followed. I had traded freely received grace for a hierarchical culture of control in which I was happy to participate because I was situated near the top.

Fear, control and a primal instinct for survival are the continuing forces driving religion forward. Religion keeps things pretty cut and dry; often informing its followers to "Do it this way or die."

A faith based in grace makes space for the question-askers and the truth-seekers while also accepting and embracing all others as well. There is no ultimatum; there is no in or out.

We're all just children of God. We're already in, and that inclusiveness allows us to love all. When we use and abuse one another, when we seek control each other, we're operating outside of an understanding of grace. When we open our hearts to one another, erasing judgments and fostering acceptance, there grace abounds.

25

REAL LIFE IS RATED "R"

I've realized that I'm living in an "R-rated world." My whole life and understanding of religion was positioned around fear of this world. It was hidden from me in my youth and warned about in my adult years.

I'm no longer afraid. I don't believe that this world will infect me. I believe that I'm here to affect and be affected, to live, and to love.

As I've written these final chapters, I have been sitting in the same Starbucks in which I made the grotesque, ungodly covenant to serve a man and his ministry for the rest of my life. The table right next to the door, where we sat on that infamous evening is gone, replaced in a recent renovation with a long bar along the window.

As I walked through the door past the place "our table" used to be, I ordered my usual, a Quad Venti, Extra Hot, Non-fat Hazelnut Latte. This was the same drink I'd held in my hands just prior to making the oath to a man that would compare in weight only to the vows I'd made with Veronica on our wedding day.

It's a Sunday morning, and on the three-minute drive from our home on my way to this particular Starbucks, I passed four churches, their parking lots full but quiet. I could imagine the vibrant church-life concealed by the front doors and foyers.

There was the faintest sense of loss as I ran through the order of service that likely all of these churches had used this morning: Opening Song, Welcome, Singing, Offering, Announcements, Sermon and Closing Song. Nothing much has changed inside those walls for several decades, and in some, nothing has changed for centuries.

Throughout the time it has taken me to live through and write about this journey, I've never come back to the scene of the crime to write. But today, on this last day of writing, it seemed appropriate to send a message to my body and my mind that the covenant that had governed my thoughts and actions was no longer applicable in my life.

It's now been over three years since it all came crashing down— our church-life, that is. We had become caught in the carnage of a violent and painful political power struggle and ended up in the fire. Slowly but surely we've come through, emerging from the smoke and ash to fly again.

Stepping out from the institutional church and into a clearer understanding of what church really is has caused me to make certain I don't just gather with like-minded hurt people and bash the church. I want to gather with, influence, and be influenced by others, have conversation with each other, and see what kind of good we can do together, independent of any organized church!

There have been many times over the last couple years where I've wanted to give up and just throw in the towel on this whole church thing! It's all so screwed up, why even try? The problems are so big, the issues so explosive, what good can possibly come of anything I do?

So many voices from the inside have asked, begged, demanded and even threatened me to not write this book. I didn't take this journey to infringe on my friends and family members who maintain a more traditional opinion of church and faith. Part of this journey has helped me reconcile my own beliefs with theirs and helped me learn to leave space for conversation and expression.

Telling my dark story of religious control and oppression has been difficult to say the least. Allowing myself to truly feel the emotions I repressed for so many years has been overwhelming at times yet so cathartic. I've found such grace and beauty hidden in the shadows, but I had to be willing to go and look for it.

It took a tenacious search for beauty to reveal beauty in all; the deeper I was willing to seek, the more I was rewarded with the complexity of beauty revealed.

For many, it's easier to continue to go about expressing their religion in the same way it's always been done, remaining content to keep their faith safe, contained in a nice, clean box to be opened on Sunday mornings.

For me, it's so much more.

My faith in God became something more than a theology, a list of beliefs and "best practices"; I began to find this divine God in every moment, in every action, everywhere... especially in the places I'd been taught he wouldn't be.

I now hold an intrinsic, even primal belief that our divine God really is everywhere and in all things. Thus, worship is the expression of the joyous discovery of all that is good and life-giving, in all aspects of life.

God is for us, for ALL of us—especially those the "church" has cast aside in judgment and condemnation. Wherever you find the outcasts, the marginalized, the sinners, there you will find Jesus, Love and the Church.

I've realized it's time for me to abandon this preoccupation with the do's and don'ts, the who's in and who's out, the rules and regulations of the religion of Christianity, and instead follow the teachings of Jesus as his message illuminates a way of life and an enlightenment of perspective that exposes the lies of religion.

When this journey beyond the doors of organized, institutionalized, regulated religion began, I spent an inordinate amount of energy railing at the church to change.

Standing just outside the walls that spanned the horizon and filled my vision, I would pound my fists against that wall until my fists were be bruised and bloodied. Not until I found the courage to step back and walk away would I find the realization that the walls of religion weren't as far reaching as I'd been led to believe.

~

After nearly three years of walking away, I can now look back from my perch on this mountaintop at the valley whence I came. I can clearly make out the four walls that contain all of the judgment, the denied hatred, the control, and the abusive spiritual hierarchies. While I was still down there, all I could see was an unbreakable, unchangeable, infinite wall, but it's now clear that I was just standing way too close to a cold, lifeless box called religion.

From my time inside that box, I knew it contained a counterfeit version of the world in which I now live. A clean, controlled environment, an imitation, a PG-rated version of life with limited impact on the rest of the world. You know one of the most exciting discoveries of my time outside that clean, sterile place? Finding that real life is rated R.

The good-boy, good-girl church drama presentation, the agenda-driven-alter-call-following performances of our youth have been replaced by visceral, emotional, heart breaking, truth-breathing, life-enhancing epics.

It both amazes and embarrasses me that we spent so many hours in debate over whether it was acceptable for a Christian to do certain things, dress a certain way, or hang out in a certain place. It also tears at my heart. We'd misunderstood the very heart and message of the gospel.

Somehow we'd interpreted "do not judge" and found justification to judge. How had we become so easily distracted from the simplicity of our faith? Jesus loves us, and so we love.

Jesus taught his followers to love God and love their neighbors as themselves. The religion we called Christianity teaches these concepts but does not properly empower us to love ourselves. Maybe the reason we don't show love to our neighbors is that we don't love ourselves. We don't know how. When we're filled with insecurity, selfishness and judgment to the point of overflow, there is no room for love.

Veronica and I are significantly stronger than we were those three years ago. We continue to try to find ways for our faith to interact with our everyday actions. When in doubt, we love. We've learned to love ourselves and love one another without judgment. We've learned to discover and love God and continue to be enthralled in the places and people where we find this loving, powerful yet misunderstood spiritual being. We've allowed ourselves to realize God is infinitely bigger than our vision and understanding had previously made room for.

I wasted many of the years leading up to my thirtieth birthday by self-limiting and allowing an inherited religion to regulate the way I experienced life. Throughout the few years since releasing myself and pursuing the fullness of life, there have been times I have nearly been overcome with shame and regret. That's where the redemptive love Jesus taught comes in to play; it is something he believed in so strongly he was willing to die for it.

Redemption is found in the forgiveness of people and the acceptance of yourself. Redemption changes the judgment of an event and thus affects the future.

Once one has experienced true and pure love, once one experiences beauty in the most intimate way, all counterfeit versions are easily identified as fraudulent imitations and discarded.

In the years to come, my faith will be a very real part of my life. The religion I once dedicated my faith to will not.

If you had to label my faith then I guess you could call me Christian, but the way I follow Jesus is wildly different than the institution that has become embroiled in pharisaic religion, where rule and regulation has overshadowed grace. Religion has hidden the life-giving beauty of grace.

The disdain I once felt towards myself for binding my future in a contract that eventually resulted in great emotional trauma is gone.

The life I once gave away has been given back to me, a second chance to love.

For a while there, I thought my time believing in God was over. If he had anything to do with this pain, then he and I were through. This journey wrecked me many, many times. On more than one occasion I found myself calling out to God, my heart screaming for answers to the emotional and relational devastation all around me.

And yet, no matter how dire the circumstances, faith, hope and love remained -- and love above all. Thought to be lost in the chaos and confusion, in the heartbreaking destruction, from the ashes love rose.

Where love is lost, death looms, but where love is found, life blooms. The kingdom of heaven is about impossible, indiscriminate love, a mindset in which love transcends the most egregious offense.

There was a fad teaching, and maybe it still exists, where churches were pushing the idea that Christianity is not a religion but a relationship. Here's the thing: religion labeled "relationship" is still religion. Jesus didn't intend to create mindless clones, but he came to reveal the inspiration and life that is already within us.

Once I erased the rules of religion that restricted my relationship with God, everything broke wide open. I now spend my life seeking love and beauty and reveling in the discovery and mystery of God in it all.

~

This journey away from religion and fear but towards the heart of God has led me to the discovery of a provocative grace that knows no bounds. At times, people have attempted to attach their disabling fears to me, as if to say, "It's better to be afraid but safe." I've learned respond with grace to those who've, knowingly or unknowingly, attempted to hamper my journey with fear. I've learned to tread boldly but walk gently.

I am thrilled as I write this. Ecstatic even. The writing of these final chapters has caused me to encounter and reveal a love that is untamed, messy and indiscriminate. It surprises me and overwhelms me even as I look across this coffee shop towards the place where I embarked on a journey that would have resulted in the silencing of this message if it weren't for the relentless, even reckless Love that destroyed my life in order to save it.

As a result of my faith shift, I no longer have a fear of death; my only fear is that I might not fully live life! Seeing, Touching, Tasting, Embracing -- a multi-sensory discovery of the fullness of the divine in it all.

I am loved by God. There is nothing I can do to change this. There is only the coming into congruence with the love that is. Understanding this love changed everything for me.

I've found the deep, authentic me and received the acceptance that was always there for me. Love whispers words of life to my heart. When these whispers of the heart are lived out in action through the body, alignment is discovered between the liminal and the seminal, between the felt and the known. I've found fulfillment in the place where intention meets action, when desire embraces deed.

While I was once lost within rules and restriction of religion, a divine Love led me back and showed me who I was, while the patient, ever-present grace of God gave me the courage to accept it.

Made in the USA
Charleston, SC
10 October 2014